AF605331

THE PHILOSOPHY OF JAZZ

KEVIN LE GENDRE

THE PHILOSOPHY OF JAZZ

First published 2025 by
The British Library
96 Euston Road
London NW1 2DB

ISBN 978 0 7123 5503 2
eISBN 978 0 7123 6869 8

Cataloguing in Publication Data
A catalogue record for this book is available from the British Library

Editorial note: in exploring the historical legacy of jazz, the author discusses racism and uses associated language thoughtfully and in context.

2 4 6 8 10 9 7 5 3 1

Represented in the EU by Authorised Rep Compliance Ltd.,
Ground Floor, 71 Lower Baggot Street, Dublin, D02 P593, Ireland.
www.arccompliance.com

Printed and bound in the Czech Republic by Finidr.

CONTENTS

INTRODUCTION

The numerous interpretations of the word 'jazz' reflect its richness and complexity. So extensive have been the changes in the music during its century-long existence that audiences for two different artists can be mutually exclusive. The question is not so much what is jazz, but why it is, and who makes this music, which is so curiously chameleon-like.

The Philosophy of Jazz reflects on the form and content as well as the sociopolitical context that frames an innovative art. The sustained evolution of jazz over the decades stems from the genius if not courage of its pioneers – strong-willed individuals willing to defy convention in order to create a musical language that has had an immeasurable influence on the course of twentieth-century culture as well as music. Many forward-thinking classical and rock artists have reinvigorated their sound through the adoption of the rhythms and timbres of jazz, while everyone from perfume makers to car manufacturers have used the word to assign sophistication to their lifestyle products.

Because the music has such a vast number of exponents, present and past, it is impossible to offer

comprehensive coverage of them all in a concise study such as this book, which comprises a number of observations on what I consider to be interesting characteristics of jazz, along with insights into the intents and purposes of notable artists.

I focus by and large on North Americans, and the relative absence of important figures from South America, Africa, Asia, Europe and the Caribbean is simply due to the aforesaid constraint. Brazilian guitarist Egberto Gismonti, South African vocalist Tutu Puoane, German saxophonist Angelika Niescier or Jamaican trumpeter Dizzy Reece could have been included. And so too could *countless* others from across the globe. International Jazz Day is an annual event that also happens every day.

The book is in three parts: 'Now' considers the music and motivations of contemporary players, some of whom may not be necessarily associated with jazz but are notable practitioners. 'Then' offers a historical overview (rather than a complete history) to provide greater context, though the onus is not on legendary figures who have been largely covered in numerous biographies and documentaries, above all the '1959 *annus mirabilis* heroes', from Miles Davis and John Coltrane to Charles Mingus, Ornette Coleman and Dave Brubeck. I willingly acknowledge their stature but have chosen to focus on other individuals whose contributions have in some cases been largely overlooked. Jazz has an abundance of histories, not a single history.

Finally, 'Now and Then, and Then and Now' assesses the fascinating relationship between past and present in jazz, or the way statements from one era echo into another so that a continuum forms, revealing not just the value of what has already been played, but its anticipation of what is yet to be played. In 2025 the legendary drummer-activist Max Roach's landmark album from 1960, *We Insist! Freedom Now Suite*, has been used as a platform for exciting work by drummer Terri Lyne Carrington and singer Christie Dashiell. Something timeless has become something else in our time.

CHAPTER ONE NOW

CREOLE MACHINA

Rather than use the word 'jazz' to describe his music Max Roach said that it belonged to a 'universe of vibrations'.[1] That was where he told stories. Sound was his language. Today the players he has inspired are creating new narratives, reflecting on their lives and making observations on the state of the world, a process that requires countless hours in rehearsal rooms and on stage. They are commited to their instruments.

Drums, piano, bass, saxophone, trumpet, trombone, flute, guitar. Maybe the voice. Possibly a laptop or loop station. One can add to that short list vibraphone, cello, violin, tuba, sitar and harp, all less common but no less interesting. Today there is an enormous variety of groups in which all these tools appear, from duos and trios to quartets, quintets and sextets, perhaps even bigger line-ups. Such as an orchestra.

Usually comprising twelve, fifteen or more pieces, this 'little army', with its 'sections' of brass, woodwinds and rhythm (drums, bass, piano, keyboards, occasionally guitar), sometimes also features a vocalist and an array of percussion instruments.

Currently there are many fine examples of the jazz big band. Trinidadian trumpeter Etienne Charles leads the Creole Orchestra, which draws on calypso, soul and R&B, and also uses turntables and cuatro, a four-string guitar used in Caribbean folk music.

The American saxophonist Steve Lehman collaborated with the Orchestre National de Jazz, a state-funded French big band, on *Ex-Machina*, an

album full of intricate, danceable polyrhythms, a mighty low end created by the use of tuba and basset horn – an early form of bass clarinet – and ghostly, murky electronic textures.

As for Orrin Evans's Captain Black Big Band, it has a deeply soulful, gospel warmth. Javier Nero's Jazz Orchestra presents a lush, tapestry-like sound often invigorated by Afro-Latin rhythms. Maria Schneider's large ensemble is a vehicle for articulate, ornate composing that features some of the best soloists in New York, while Jon Irabagon's *Server Farm* combo is invigorating for its wily blend of acoustic and electric timbres, glitch-like soundscapes and hard funk-rock grooves, all of which frame a thought-provoking question on the considerable challenges posed by artificial intelligence.

All of the above are of tremendous importance because of the possibilities they afford composers and players who want to create music that has a rich palette of tonal colour and harmonic detail. They enable interesting improvisations that will grow from material that is handled with discipline, so that the large resources, the rows of horns and the 'engine' of the rhythm section somehow become one. The challenge is not to be taken lightly. The sonic-dramatic range of an orchestra, its potential for intimacy as well as high energy, enables jazz artists to fulfil a key tenet of the music: ambition.

Big bands lead to the materialization of sounds that may have been in a composer's mind. The chords used by a trio could be scored for more instruments that bring vivid imagery to the fore. Timbres further brighten and darken, textures harden and soften, decibel levels rise and fall. While small groups greatly appeal to improvisers for their structural flexibility, the chance to 'scale up' can engage the imagination in new ways.

'You have all those different voices, different colours that can be so detailed and we also have the electronic component to reinforce the implications of some of those colours,' says Steve Lehman. 'It's an interesting balance. With a big band the emphasis shifts. It's more of a collective effort, with a spotlight on different players.'[2]

As far as Javier Nero is concerned, the greater means available – the additional horns in particular – inspire him as a writer–arranger. 'It allows my music to reach the highest and lowest extremes dynamically, and also allows me to expand the compositions in ways that would be too demanding or challenging in a smaller group setting.'[3]

Furthermore the orchestra is a symbol of unity and community. It is a dozen or more players bound by common cause, sometimes celebrating the history of jazz, as in the case of Britain's Nu Civilisation Orchestra's sublime tribute to Duke Ellington (a founding father of the music), or the Sun Ra Arkestra (born in the 1950s), who offer a unique living history of jazz. Carriers of yesterday, they could not be more today.

OUT OF ONE, MANY BANDS

The orchestra is like a large frame that has many pictures inside. There are bands within the big band. Listening to a dozen or more musicians is stimulating because of the richness of the collective sound and the brilliance of the individuals who create it, but there are important components – units – that can also exist independently.

Most obviously there is a rhythm section at the orchestra's core. The piano trio, as in piano, double bass and drums, is one of the most common and popular types of jazz group and has numerous exponents from around the world who headline major international festivals: Craig Taborn, Myra Melford, Tyshawn Sorey, Jason Moran, Marie Krüttli, Alexander Hawkins. The saxophone quartet, in which the reed instrument is the lead backed by the aforesaid trio, also has loyal

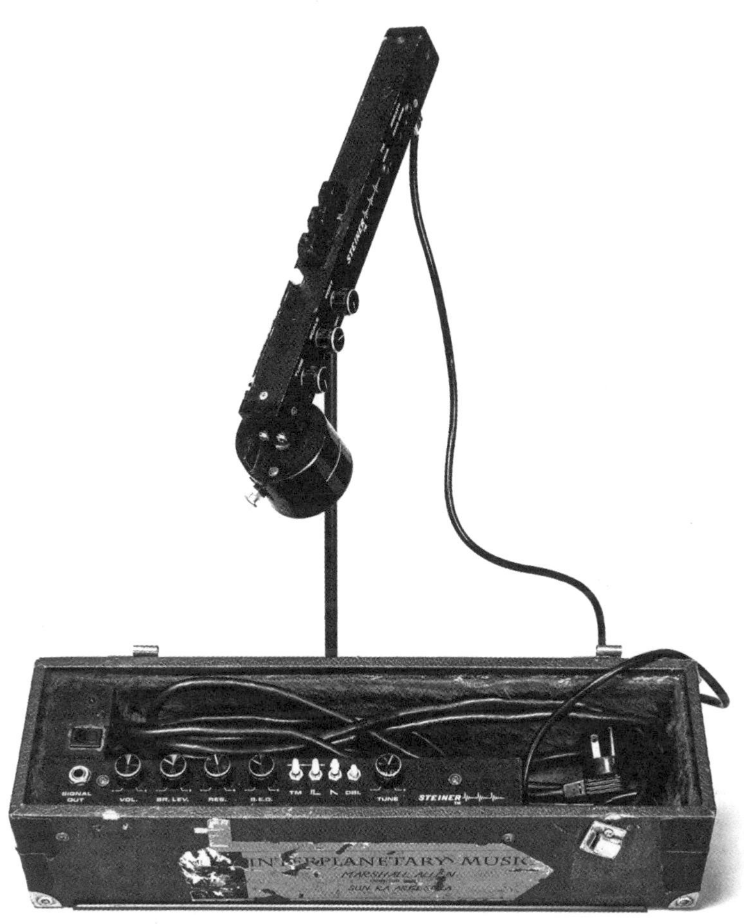
SIGNAL OUT
VOL.
BR. LEV.
RES.
TM
DBL
TUNE
STEINER

followers. Walter Smith III, David Murray, Adele Sauros and James Brandon Lewis are good examples.

However if groups are formed by building upon the piano trio and the saxophone quartet, there are also numerous bands created by paring them back, by removing an instrument. For example the saxophone trio – saxophone, double bass and drums – can be tremendously satisfying and creative because some musicians feel that the keyboard can act as a constraint, and that the absence of chords is actually liberating. The piano-less quartet, as in two horns, double bass and drums, is interesting too.

Yet there are groups in which the drums or bass drop out, leaving horn-piano-bass and horn-piano-drums, or another horn may be added to either of these line-ups.

Survey enough jazz ensembles and it soon becomes apparent that there really is no jazz band per se, but bands formed by jazz musicians according to their specific concept and ambition, and the artistic kinship they may feel with others. The combinations become more or less endless, to the extent that uncommon is a more appropriate term than unusual for the band led by saxophonist Jowee Omicil: it uses brass, reeds, bass, keys, percussion, voice and two drum kits, creating a thrillingly dense, barrelling sound that can also be ethereal, enigmatic and misty.

While the orchestral work of Etienne Charles and Steve Lehman may be highlights in their discographies, to date the work of the former in a sextet and the latter in a trio, or quartet with saxophonist Mark Turner, is excellent. The question is not so much what bands have they already led, but what kind of bands might they lead in the future.

SINGULAR NOUN, PLURAL MEANINGS

'Jazz' does not lend itself to quick and easy definitions. The word is singular but its meanings and manifestations are plural. Improvisation is often foregrounded in debates on the music, but equally important are the intriguing, mutable relationship it has with composition, the interplay between these two concepts, and how any assumed hierarchy of structural elements can be challenged, so that rhythm can have as much narrative importance as melody, or maybe rhythmic melody can prevail. What makes a tune is open to debate.

Also interesting are: the relationship between individual and collective, the varying interpretation of the roles of leader and accompanist according to specific bands; the exchanges of ideas that can occur between musicians, the conversational richness; the changing function of a player, so that a saxophonist may act as a drummer or bassist, or all ensemble members play percussively; a single performer being so multi-faceted in approach they acquire the expressive range of a whole band; the engaging moment when a soloist is taking off, or indeed reining in, being creative as much by subtraction as addition of notes; the magical sensation of several players locking in together to create 'groove', a kind of pooled, carefully coordinated energy.

The highest standards of musicianship, including listening skills, facilitate this. Yet the more abstract

quality of *feel* – how a player can catch the ear, if not stir the soul, by way of nuance, the slightest variation of weight, attack or timing of a note – is also pivotal.

And the risk taken by artists, the courage to pursue ideas and translate feelings into sound when there is no guarantee the outcome will resonate with others, matters too. As do wholly personal interpretations, or indeed transformations of known material, be it a current pop song, a classical theme or a standard from the jazz canon. Freedom of expression is all.

Rooted in African-American history, lived experience, intellect, imagination and folklore, jazz in its lifespan of just over a hundred years has been so dynamic it has taken myriad forms, or grown several metaphorical branches from a complex foundational tree. One could perceive jazz as an art that lives in and moves between acoustic and electric worlds, often becoming electro-acoustic in resonance due to the range of instruments deployed, as has been the case in one of its principal sources: the blues.

A vast range of approaches to rhythm, be it cyclical, circular, swinging or backbeat-driven, and harmony, whether tonal, polytonal, atonal, microtonal or contrapuntal, is deployed by contemporary jazz artists. And rather than opting for either one of these methods, they may use many – if not all – according to what they set out to achieve in their narratives. A musician may play time, changing time or no time. They may deploy African-American, Cuban, Brazilian, European or Asian sources – or any beat and folk tune from anywhere (indeed players applying local cultural knowledge and life experience is paramount). The point is to create newness and to find points of invention from existing conventions, which often involves treading the line between what is *proper* or improper sound.

In any case artists draw on a past marked by evolution, consolidation and innovation. Perhaps the real concern is the thinking behind sound. Indeed, the restlessness of the jazz aesthetic means investigation and research of the highest order so that artists might eschew as much as accept established methods. The wholly original music of saxophonist Steve Lehman stems from his strong rhythmic base and bold use of low register, largely under the inspiration of such role models as Henry Threadgill, the Pulitzer Prize-winning composer who has written intricate, earthy, otherwordly music since the late 1960s. Lehman made an important conceptual choice for his 2023 *Ex Machina* project. He found an alternative to composition on the basis of chords:

I have this idea of thinking about harmony in terms of frequency relationships, like the amount of times a soundwave is vibrating in a second. In the best-case scenario it can open up some really interesting possibilities for how to build harmonies that use different types of tunings than we're used to in the Western system. It's a way of working with harmony that can present some new elements and new ways of thinking about dissonance and consonance.

He adds: 'That abstraction and intellectual inquiry with the harmony, there's a long history of that going hand in hand with the same kind of sophistication rhythmically that manifests as something that feels danceable.'[4] The serious is not incompatible with the joyous.

To the physical and cerebral one might add the emotional: the jazz ballad. Love songs, in which artists address affairs of the heart through profoundly charged instrumental or vocal themes, are also part of the music's eclectic character, though some players are minded to investigate many forms of love, from the platonic and parental to the spiritual and divine, as well as the romantic. Past and present songs such as 'Body and Soul', 'Acknowledgement', 'Beatrice', 'Tell Me', 'Just the Two of Us', 'You Move Me', 'All Matter', 'Three Gifts (From a Nigerian Mother to God)' and 'Black Iris'[5] speak of the substantial metaphysical and cultural complexity of responses to an eternal question: what are these things called love?

The music also has an enduring relationship with a whole range of other art forms such as painting, cinema, television, choreography, theatre, spoken word and poetry.

And jazz can be sociopolitical. It addresses a range of subjects that relate to the human condition, and as an instrumental and vocal form, it makes statements that are implicit and explicit, requiring listeners to fully engage. If saxophonist Darius Jones evokes alienation and trauma on 'We Outside', then bassist Reggie Washington and singers Ezra Schwarz-Bart and Stephanie McKay of the Black Lives Collective make the point on 'I Apologize' that the post-George Floyd world has not yet delivered the much longed-for racial equality, as the subject slips down the mainstream media agenda. And vocalist Candice Hoyes, percussionist Val Jeanty and bassist Mimi Jones of the group Nite Bjuti tell vivid stories about the lives of Black women in the twenty-first century, aware of their African-Caribbean and African-American heritage, which is channelled into imaginative soundscapes.

The word 'jazz' has long been – and still is – viewed with ambivalence by many artists who prefer descriptors such as creative or improvised music. But it is largely seen as an umbrella term for several sub-genres: straight-ahead or post-bop is largely acoustic and swing-based; jazz-rock or fusion is largely electric; soulful or R&B-flavoured jazz sometimes has a hip-hop flavour; spiritual jazz has devotional and mantra-like moods; Latin jazz is often centred on layers of percussion and African belief systems; and avant-garde, where approaches to composition can be abstract and non-linear, moves away from the model of a stated theme and solo. But any particular school with which an individual may be linked ultimately matters far less than the individual or the personal language they are able to fashion from the vocabularies they use or develop.

TAPE HEADS

All the above schools have notable exponents, be it saxophonist Branford Marsalis, one of the most distinguished straight-ahead players of his generation or pianist Matthew Shipp, an irrepressible giant of the avant-garde, or the group Butcher Brown, whose irresistibly funky sound is enhanced by Afrobeat grooves, electronics and the versatility of frontman Tennishu, who plays saxophone and trumpet – and raps.

But there are many artists whose desire to use their extensive knowledge of the whole history of jazz in unpredictable ways makes them pleasingly hard to classify, so that they either move liberally between styles or end up creating something in which there are echoes of the past rather than obvious retreads of it. For example, the Cuban pianist David Virelles makes original music using improvisation, Afro-Cuban rhythms and folklore that feel both ancient and futuristic, showing how traditional percussion such as guataca, conga and clavé are entirely relevant to his unique compositional world.

First and foremost, the most interesting improvising artists have great attention to detail, which can mean a focus on a very specific timbre. Examples include the harpsichord played by Phillip Golub in his deeply mysterious, mutative songs or the bells used by trumpeter and multi-instrumentalist Ben LaMar Gay alongside drums, guitar and tuba to create an entrancing, ceremonial music that often floats and hovers on the pulse.

And there can also be humour in the way a contemporary jazz musician writes a song that has an interesting ambiguity in structure, which can feel fluid rather than rigid, pushing and pulling the listener's perceptions in a number of different directions.

For example, the title track of South Korean bassist Jeong Lim Yang's 2025 album *Synchronicity* is a charming feat of rhythmic and harmonic trickery that stems from both her imagination and the skill of an excellent band (viola player Mat Maneri, pianist Jacob Sacks and drummer Randy Peterson.) A repeated piano riff is heard going in and out of time, the line slipping off centre, swaying between beats to create a sense of subtle displacement that is emphasized by the drums and two string instruments that also shift around the implied pulse. Irregular regularity and regular irregularity. There is a minorish cry in the sound, and a hint of out-of-tune-ness to match the out-of-time-ness, but the construct still holds together amid the mild flux, the wavering. Attempting to count the movement of quavers (eighth notes) across a single measure is not uninteresting, but allowing oneself to be teased by their whimsical progress, marshalled with great skill by the band, is where the real satisfaction lies. The effect is almost like that of an old cassette tape tantalizingly fraying, slowing and distorting to create a mischievous frailty, as the C30–C60–C90 generation will know only too well.

PANHANDLING

All of the aforementioned artists are part of the modern-day landscape of jazz. Their numerous recordings, appearances at festivals and presence in the specialist and occasionally mainstream media grow audiences and further our understanding of how the music is developing. They use established vocabularies to create new ones.

Yet as much as we value the experience of hearing creative excellence on piano, voice, saxophone, drums or trumpet, one should also recognize jazz made on other instruments, because the music is a set of ideas that transcend any specific sound. Hence there is immense value in a great if largely unheralded soloist playing what is a 'street thing'. Some have mockingly called it 'the big salad bowl'. It is a steel pan.

Despite the prevailing image of the steel pan as a vehicle for simple folk tunes, it is a prime source for jazz because of the textural richness, rhythmic drive and dramatic changes of mood it generates in the hands of players who are also masters of the art of improvisation. For those who may ask where a reclaimed oil drum (a device once maligned by British colonial authorities) belongs, all they need to do is lend an ear to 'pannist' Leon Foster Thomas. His answer is in a quartet or an orchestra. Thomas is enviably versatile. When playing his own compositions with his Calasanitus band he can be intensely lyrical, making it clear that the steel pan is as much a vehicle for contemplative, heartfelt melody as it is upbeat dance rhythm. The instrument can evoke a mysterious, haunting darkness and bright, balmy sweetness.

But the question of artistic legitimacy endures, as he recalls. 'There are people who just don't think that steel pan is a serious instrument.'[6] That is a statement of great magnitude when one considers that the critical establishment said the same thing about the first jazz drum kits over a century ago. This disheartening repeated history is a pointed reminder that jazz artists today stand on the shoulders of giants who bravely faced down prejudice from power brokers who misunderstood their inventions.

'Some universities didn't accept my application because I played steel pan. I had to get in as a percussion major', Thomas says of his struggles with American music education bureaucracy. He was born in Trinidad and has lived in Miami and London.

Synonymous with working-class Black Caribbean culture, namely carnival and street parades, the steel pan is one of the youngest acoustic instruments in the world. Its genesis dates back to the 1930s, but it has a unique timbre that falls somewhere between the chime of a glockenspiel and the tingle of a vibraphone. A virtuoso such as Thomas impugns the notion that pan is not a proper jazz instrument and supplants it with the reality that jazz is made on any given instrument if the player is capable. Remember that what now passes as a classic jazz instrument, the saxophone, was not born so in the 1840s but was incrementally developed into one over time. And that the harp would not be in jazz today had Dorothy Ashby and Alice Coltrane not brought their improvisational-compositional vision to it in the 1950s and 1960s. Instruments are used in jazz, but jazz is not reducible to instruments.

When Thomas appeared at Soul Mama in London in 2024 as a special guest of his compatriot Etienne Charles's Creole Orchestra (discussed earlier), he took a solo that left the audience utterly spellbound. He lit a proverbial fire under the band. That he was performing calypso, jazz, funk or calypso jazz-funk was not the point. Conversant with the multitude of rhythms associated with those genres, from fluttery, airy swing to bulky, heavy backbeats, Thomas produced a maelstrom of sounds, some melodic, some counter-melodic, some percussive, some disruptive, some harshly aggressive, some deeply hypnotic. Idea upon idea upon idea brought an energy rush. An uninterrupted flow was marked by great phrasal

variety, a lengthening, contracting, subdividing of lines, changes of attack and accenting of notes, skips between sparkling quavers (eighths) and glinting semiquavers (sixteenths) and shifts of timbre that created a wide spectrum of colour that moved from bright to glow to mute within a few beats. At one point, volleys of triplets came in such quick succession they almost crashed into one another, unleashing a vigorously propulsive effect that sent shockwaves around the room, enhanced by gradual ascents in pitch, a climb upwards like a gymnast's somersault, the moment the body gracefully twists after a leap in the air.

In collaborations between classical orchestras and jazz ensembles the violinists from the former usually raise an eyebrow in awe when they hear the saxophonists from the latter improvise, but this time round it was the reed section that gasped as Thomas did his thing. If only an American University admissions officer had been in the house.

Another fascinating concert in which he took part in London, at the Vortex club, was with Black Top, the avant-garde British duo comprising pianist Pat Thomas and vibraphonist Orphy Robinson, with a unique modus operandi. They create music spontaneously at every live performance, featuring different collaborators who are minded to both take the lead and respond to the stimulus that occurs on the night. The band becomes a new band every time it invites a new guest to the stage. There is no set list, no rehearsal and no expectation but the sound of the unexpected.

Apart from piano and vibraphone, Thomas and Robinson use an arsenal of electronic equipment including samplers, loop stations and sequencers to create a barrage of beats and effects that can make the music densely layered and strangely, stimulatingly textured. Robinson recalls being astounded by the strength of Thomas's contributions – from his driving riffs to the precision of his note manipulation – to the extent that he duly forgot that the pan was an acoustic device bobbing away in an electric swamp.

This ambiguity is an advantage. When performing with Black Top, alongside other guests, vocalist-emcee Cleveland Watkiss and turntablist Mariam Rezaei,

Thomas added to a blurring of lines between what might be pure and impure, natural and unnatural, clean and dirty, ugly and beautiful, pleasing and displeasing, by aligning tones that suggest a machine and tones created by a machine. Sound was mystery.

I'd been a fan of avant-garde music for a long time; the freedom to explore is what I appreciate. You didn't know what was coming next, you picked up on things and went with the synergy on stage. And I could also create interesting effects in the way I held the sticks, which really fitted in with the electronics. The bottom end, the warmth of the pan also seemed to work well in that context.

Thomas embodies subversion in jazz, his ability to be as effective in an orchestral setting as he is in a freely improvised one forces a rethink of his instrument. Steel pan is a folk device from the analogue era that is well suited to high art in the digital age.

BOOTY SHAKIN' BASSMAN

Leon Foster Thomas is the link between Etienne Charles's Creole Orchestra and Black Top, and the contrast between the two groups could not be greater. That is a sign of the idiomatic breadth of contemporary jazz, its spectrum running from swing to avant-garde, tight time to loose time, written songs to spur-of-the-moment sound. It is possible that he had very different audiences at the aforementioned concerts.

Interestingly, the net result of all this activity is that contemporary jazz has apparent polar opposites that sometimes elide in thrilling ways. One of the most appealing aspects of a group like Black Top, whether collaborating with Thomas, saxophonists Steve Williamson and Xhosa Cole or guitarist Jean-Paul Bourelly, is its flexibility.

The players use a blank canvas, or an 'open sky' as some say, in order to trawl through a number of timbres or tonal areas. Sometimes fleetingly suggesting one, and in a precise moment a trigger will be found for a complete rhythm that can be held then quickly abandoned to be replaced by another, or developed into a more substantial theme like modelling clay squeezed into shapes of different sizes. There is liquidity in the music, yet it can suddenly solidify into a driving dance groove, often with an implication of the shadowy, skulking character of Jamaican dub.

The way that these unscripted motifs emerge from a sea of sound is exciting, underlining the fact that improvisation can lead to moments of composition that are ultimately teased out and not telegraphed. They will arrive when they are meant to.

A strong folk sensibility can also enhance this high standard of musicianship and use of powerful creative reflexes. For example, the mesmerizing drummer Francisco Mela is a player of extraordinary skill who is part of a quartet with saxophonist Daniel Carter, bassist William Parker and pianist Leo Genovese. While Mela's polyrhythmic ability is appropriate for the spontaneous music-making of the group, he also occasionally sings traditional Cuban melodies at what he feels are the right moments, bringing an ancestral, lyrical character to bear on the daring exploration of sound.

This kind of music is usually filed under experimental or avant-garde, but it is really a profound form of communication or a wide-ranging conversation between individuals that often brings into pay much timeless cultural information as well as technical skill. Mela is an archetype of the musician who really challenges perceptions of his identity. Fully engaging with his Cuban heritage, he is creating a kind of folk art.

As exciting as the above are there is also something vital about what might be called the more accessible end of jazz. A theme and a solo are long-standing strategies, but they are not outdated. The question is how well can they be applied? American vocalist Michael Mayo is a prime example of an artist performing beautiful melodies – originals and standards – with enormous textural and emotional richness. At his most interesting Mayo moves between understatement and emphasis, and his ability to take a composition such as Herbie Hancock's 'Butterfly' from ethereal grace to impassioned energy shows a real command of dynamics and dramatic light and shade. Whether using a loop station to create a choir and rhythm section from multiple sung and live-sampled parts or swinging hard with his *real* rhythm section, Mayo has an ingenuity and personality that could make him an important recent arrival in jazz.

One could also point to a plethora of artists who write deeply lyrical compositions that they enhance with strong, expressive soloing that touches listeners.

A great melody is, after all, a precious thing. It could be stated by saxophonist Joshua Redman, pianist Aaron Diehl or vocalists Cécile McLorin Salvant and Bilal. It can be four, eight, eleven or thirteen bars of compelling, affecting sound, shaped by precise inflection that can stand with or without chords. The way saxophonist-bass clarinettist Marcus Strickland blends hard-edged beats, live playing and haunting melodic choruses on his *Nihil Novi* album, a deft amalgam of jazz, soul, funk and hip-hop, is noteworthy. But hearing artists perform live adds another dimension to their work. A well-

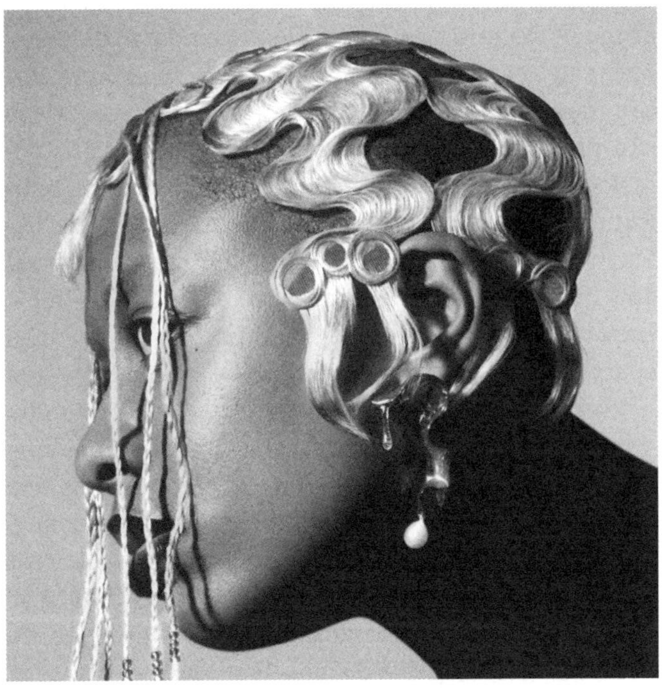

recorded CD can be a faithful chronicle of repertoire – at least part of it – but there is another level of detail to be appreciated at a concert.

A musician such as bassist Christian McBride always wins over audiences with the immense invention, precision and momentum of his lines. This is especially noteworthy when he plays with a highly responsive and intuitive drummer such as Brian Blade, or in the great beauty of his tone on a ballad – especially moving when heard unamplified in a venue with exceptional acoustics such as Wigmore hall in London. McBride's absolute command of his instrument is astounding, but equally important is the bold, buoyant personality that he brings to every one of his performances. His engagement with Black popular culture is strong, as is his pride in his native Philadelphia, a city with a vibrant history of soul, funk and hip-hop as well as jazz.

As much as he maintains the highest standards of musicianship and artistry, McBride does not deny his formative years playing for dances in a high school big band, where the songbook included pop-soul star Whitney Houston and swing icon Count Basie. This means that he may end a gig by chanting 'It's time to shake your booty.' And when he sings that – in a booming, baritone voice – people do as they are told.

FEELING THE SPIRIT

All of the above may bid us to consider the changing nature of sound, song, composition, improvisation, rhythm and the possibility of bodily response to music.

It is fascinating to think about how these elements are developed in jazz, but of equal importance is *why*. The feelings, the thoughts, the worldview, convictions and beliefs of the artist – their life experiences – shape the stories told with sound and word.

That happens in literal terms at performances by the inspirational South African pianist Nduduzo Makhathini, who might break a set of great musical beauty – in which he plays chorale-like melodies and rhythms that have all the organic intricacy of breathing patterns – to make a lengthy speech about the richness of Zulu cosmology and ritual, and the deployment of Black ancestral practice as an anti-colonial force.

As for saxophonist Wilkins, a Philadelphia native, he predicated his masterful 2023 album *The Seventh Hand* on African-American and Afro-diasporic spiritual practices such as Yoruba culture, and Santería, where complex ancestral drums play a trance-like beat that is wilfully used to summon one or several deities.

In the process he built a bold, coherent bridge between composition and improvisation. 'A lot of music is based on my experience in the Black church and discourse around what purpose it serves in the community,' says Wilkins, whose tone and phrasing can move from floating serenity to molten intensity in an instant.

It became about spirit possession and what it would mean for me to write a suite of seven pieces that allowed us to be vessels for God. Each movement develops until the last one is pretty much all improvised, there's no written material as such. You're called upon to be

a vessel. What we call this in the Black church is the baptism of the Holy Spirit. Community is a big part of it... a non-ego-centred way of sharing, like a gathering.

In performance at Ronnie Scott's in London in 2023, Wilkins's quartet was hugely impressive. The theme of spirit possession that defines *The Seventh Hand* brought profound emotion to the music; and the sustained intensity of the suite, the relentless polyrhythmic drive, the dense but agile harmony and a constant build of stark, vivid tension over a lengthy duration, held a packed house quite enthralled.

THE ONE AND THE MANY

An online broadcast of Wilkins at Dia Chelsea Art Gallery in New York, where he performed solo, interpreting a score realized by visual artists Leslie Hewitt and Jamal Cyrus, was also a revelation for the way he showed a side of character that was more meditative and less expansive, but no less impressive. That movement from a stage where he led others to one where he expressed himself without them is interesting.

Ultimately, the player and instrument *are* the band. The soloist with the orchestra in their heads. The soloist who emerges from an ensemble as well as merges with it. The soloist who may have the audacity to use a chordal or a single-note instrument, a piano saxophone, bass clarinet, flute or trumpet to improvise a concert for an hour or more.

One musician may think as a rhythm or horn section. A pianist can be more obviously orchestral because of the range of a keyboard, but other players do not have to feel limited, as saxophonist Rudresh Mahanthappa – a key exponent of the instrument since the late 1990s – explains by recalling a vital lesson he had with Joe Lovano, a major figure on the instrument since the 1980s. 'We looked at a piece for quartet and he said I should be able play on my horn *all* the parts I'd written for drums, bass, piano, guitar, whatever. I had to think like *I* was the group, not just a saxophonist.'[7]

And then there was one. Without a band, some artists can thrive alone in concert. Among the contemporary players who have risen to the challenge, apart from

Wilkins, are Ambrose Akinmusire, Arve Henriksen, Lionel Loueke, Angelica Sanchez, Satoko Fujii, Sam Newsome, Ava Mendoza, Sylvie Courvoisier and Marco Colonna, to name but some. These horn players, guitarists and pianists have performed solo in clubs, concert halls, castles, churches and breweries, and have such a breadth of ideas on phrasing, harmony, timbre and pulse that their respective characters – all very different – can evoke joyous, vigorous motion, contemplative stillness, the crash and clatter of the mechanized world, the chirp and chatter of the animal kingdom. They take a focused journey through sound in which every line – sometimes a single note – can be a mini-event. If the big band with its twelve or fifteen players is an orchestra of many, then the solo jazz artist is a distant but important cousin: an orchestra of one.

CHAPTER TWO THEN

WIDE OPEN

If the idea of a contemporary jazz musician being able to play so expressively he becomes an orchestra of one is interesting then it is by no means new. Improvising artists have been thinking along those lines since the start of the twentieth century – the infancy of the music – and a statement to that effect made by a legendary figure carries particular currency: 'The piano should always be an imitation of a jazz band.'[8]

So said Jelly Roll Morton in 1919. His strong rhythmic left hand and restless, roaming right hand did indeed make him a highly expressive player, a gifted improviser and a canny composer who published songs that were hugely influential. But perhaps more importantly he embodied a spirit of rampant creativity among Creole and African-American musicians. In the 1890s, not yet thirty years after the abolition of slavery, ragtime had been pioneered by, among others, pianist Scott Joplin, in which jumpy offbeats producing jolts of energy over a steady march-like two-four pulse caught the ear of audiences in America, and also enshrined Black colloquialism as a notable phenomenon. Ragtime is a diminutive of 'raggedy time', a humorous expression for an approach to rhythm that is playful, if not whimsical.

'The beat is wide.' Older African-American artists, some of whom grew up learning both Morton and Joplin's sheet music, have made this point on numerous occasions. Conceptually, they were reflecting on the importance of placing accents in unusual places, and syncopation as a source of excitement and invigoration

as well as an organizing principle, which produced a slew of remarkable songs in the late 1910s and early 1920s.

The buoyant energy of Joplin's 'Maple Leaf Rag' is also matched by a compositional ambition that saw him give the piece numerous clearly defined sections that are like mini-chapters in a story. Morton exercised similar imagination on his solo works and pieces for

ensemble such as 'Black Bottom Stomp', where he deploys his septet in ever-changing configurations, scaling down and up so the band reveals micro-bands. Structurally, the song is a marvel for its use of melody and countermelody, blend of two and four-beat lines, slides between pitches, and spry, 'stomping' rhythms.

And the instruments used in early jazz carried history. Derived from the ngoni, the West African string instrument found in Senegal and Mali, the banjo, yielding percussive, pentatonic rhythms, was widely played by African slaves and minstrel troupes. They were imitated and racially caricatured by white musicians in America in the 1800s, while the cornet, trombone and tuba came from European brass bands, and the clarinet, violin and double bass from classical orchestras.

As for the drum kit, it was one of the most important elements of early jazz bands insofar as it was an invented, improvised, noisy, controversial instrument, borne of the desire to take rhythmic devices from a marching band - bass drum, snare and hi-hat cymbal - and assemble them as a single entity played by one musician. The thinking was ingenious.

But the mindset of the African Americans who were developing forms of music in its first stage was one of resourcefulness. They used anything from combs and kazoos to jugs, fifes and washboards, as if they had signed up to an unofficial manifesto of which the primary clause was 'sound by any means necessary.'

Although cities such as St. Louis, Chicago, Kansas, Detroit, Los Angeles and New York are important in jazz history, the key hub was New Orleans, a unique cultural crossroads in America. It was there that the blend of African, native American, Caribbean, French and Spanish influences produced a dazzling mosaic of music, language, religion and ritual. The classic New Orleans jazz sound had raucous, joyous polyphony, swirling counterpoint, and 'stop time' for concise punchy riffs, while a range of social dances, such as the foxtrot and two-step, accompanied the music.

Birthplace of Morton, the city was also home to a large number of other influential musicians, notably cornet-trumpet players from Buddy Bolden and Freddie Keppard to King Oliver and Louis Armstrong. He was one of the first major soloists in what became known as jazz, from 'jass' – a Black colloquialism for sex, which consolidated the idea that the music was fit for the 'sporting houses' (brothels) in the Crescent City.

Armstrong's remarkably powerful, lustrous tone, his command of the upper register, the tremendous tonal colour he produced by scooping notes as well as playing them clean, not to mention his 'hot' rhythmic drive, all stemmed from his extreme dedication to his craft as well as his talent. His wordless, or scat vocal was also enthralling, but Armstrong developed a kind of total expression which saw him move spontaneously from short brass riffs to longer solos to melodic singing to informal, intimate spoken word, as if he wanted to address the listener in a personal way. This produced deeply poignant performances such as '(What Did I Do to Be So) Black and Blue'.[9] Although it is called a foxtrot on the label of the 1929 recording, this was a key anti-racism song.

LOUIS ARMSTRONG

KIND OF BLUES

Like several other soloists, Armstrong played with many female singers, notably Victoria Spivey, Hociel Thomas and Lillie Delk Christian, who were exponents of a major constituent part not just of jazz but of modern Western pop: the blues.

The likes of Ma Rainey, Mamie Smith and Bessie Smith – dubbed 'The Empress of the Blues' – were also pivotal figures in the evolution of a phenomenon that was much more than music. The blues is about stance, outlook, worldview, and psychological and emotional self-preservation as much as it is a skilled manipulation of notes and tones. It is about thinking, feeling and playing, or bidding others to think and feel as one plays, with honesty and vulnerability as well as self-assertion and daring mischief.

Considering that up until the 1860s anti-literacy laws prohibited slaves from learning to read and write, and that equality in public education remained a battleground for decades post emancipation, what African Americans have achieved with language is remarkable. The startling ingenuity of the rich turns of phrase and neologisms of the blues is a prime example of an influential minority group that has grown in word just as it had grown in sound. The blues can reveal the extraordinary in the ordinary, and the wit and wonder of folk tales.

The blues has irony, simile and metaphor that the finest poet would envy, so if a guitarist wants to ridicule a pianist with a lyric he does it by telling him not that his upright is all broke down but that the piano ain't nothin' but a guitar in a coffin. And if Bessie Smith, in her forceful, affecting voice, wanted to boast of her erotic power she did so by saying 'Nobody in Town Can Bake A Sweet Jelly Roll Like Mine', which has more sassy, coded imagination and provocation than explicitly bragging about the tastiest part of her person.

The lack of shame on the subject of sexuality as well as love made the blues a vital secular complement to the sacred song of the negro spiritual, whose subject matter is restricted to all things godly rather than earthly. Rooted in southern Black culture, the blues has a 'cry', or deeply expressive pitch-bending 'wail', call-and-response and the specific harmony of minor thirds, fifths and sevenths, and though the twelve-bar form became one of the most common models of the blues, the music can also played in cycles of eight, ten, eleven or thirteen as long as musical verve and emotional honesty are upheld. Then again, an individual talking over just one chord can also be a compelling blues.

If there was a raw, tough character to 1920s and 1930s blues lyrics, jazz musicians evoked vigour if not violence in sound. The brilliant but unheralded pianist Sam Goold wrote 'Whipping the Keys' and the more famous Fats Waller penned 'Smashing Thirds'. And the idea of motion, of propulsion and push forward, defined techniques and associated language. Ragtime piano gave way to 'stride', whereby more complex left-hand patterns – sometimes with intervals of tenths rather than octaves – invigorated tunes and bassists began to 'stroll' or 'walk', marking all four beats of a bar. This facilitated the evolution from two-four to four-four time, and the principle of 'swing' took hold, with its subtle variations of attack ahead and behind the beat producing a sense of balanced tension and steady momentum that excited listeners and dancers.

When pianist-bandleader Duke Ellington wrote 'It Don't Mean a Thing (If it Ain't Got That Swing)' he enshrined the idea of music that was predicated on strong rhythm that equalled the value of melody or harmony. Although he played in small groups, Ellington, along with other composers both Black (Fletcher Henderson, Chick Webb, Count Basie) and white (Paul Whiteman, Artie Shaw, Benny Goodman), became a major figurehead of the orchestra that comprised between twelve and fifteen players. They typically featured a rhythm section, trumpets, trombones and saxophones, and occasionally singers (the innovative Billie Holiday, Chick Bullock, Ella Fitzgerald), and played a form of dance music, often with purring vibrato, driving beat, stabbing riffs and 'shout choruses' that packed ballrooms and inspired steps such as the lindy hop, the jitterbug and the shim-sham.

Ellington's impact in Europe was huge and the arrival of foreign talents such as the innovative Belgian guitarist Django Reinhardt, with whom he would tour, enshrined jazz as an international art form that would continue to grow around the world.

Yet America was still in the grip of segregation and the phenomenon of 'race records', whereby jazz and blues songs were deemed, first and foremost, to be products for negro consumers. If that policy reflected division, then explicitly discriminatory language – shocking by today's standards – was to be found in mainstream literature. This showed that for all white America's embrace of 'hot' music, Black jazz musicians were still subject to racial slurs reminiscent of the days of minstrel troupes, as evidenced in Ernest Hemingway's *The Sun Also Rises*, which depicts hedonistic white Americans at boozy play in Europe: 'The nigger drummer waved at

SACK
AMUSEMENT
ENTERPRISES
Presents
DUKE ELLINGTON
AND HIS
COTTON CLUB ORCHESTRA
in
BLACK AND TAN
with
FREDI WASHINGTON

Brett, we were caught in the jam, dancing in one place in front of him… he was all teeth and lips.'

The paradoxes, or rather hypocrisies, of white acceptance of Black music rather than Black people did not stop there. The most obvious manifestation was the Cotton Club in Harlem, New York, which hired Black artists while operating a whites-only door policy. It was here that Ellington established himself as a central figure in the cultural flowering of the Harlem Renaissance, with its innovations in literature and visual art as well as music. He also made vital statements of 'negro pride' on a number of songs, such as 'Black and Tan Fantasy' and 'Black Beauty', and the highly ambitious suite *Black, Brown and Beige*, which suggest that if there is a philosophy of jazz then it is about retaining dignity in the midst of a dark, dehumanizing world.

Ellington and his highly talented arranger and co-composer Billy Strayhorn created startlingly beautiful tonal canvases through their inventive approach to scoring, where they might blend a clarinet playing at the lowest end of its register with a trombone at the highest. The extraordinary musicians at their disposal – above all brass players who used deeply expressive techniques such as growls and 'wa wa' vibrato – made the music enthralling. Ellington's vast repertoire had sensual wonders such as 'The Mooche', which, like many other pieces, has become a 'standard' that contemporary jazz artists are still minded to interpret. Initially inspired by stride players, Ellington was also a fine solo pianist, and he excelled as an orchestra of one in addition to his orchestra of many.

BEBOP, R&B, BEARCATS

Curiosity and imagination drove change in jazz. The likes of Dizzy Gillespie, Charlie Christian, Charlie Parker and Max Roach helped transform swing into bebop, a controversial subgenre. It had challenging chord changes, rhythms that were more fragmented – popping with unpredictable accents on the bass drum – and lengthy themes with a jittery, jumpy character that put complex rhythm at the top of the composition as much as the bottom. Mostly working in small groups such as quartets and quintets, bebop musicians sometimes took the harmony of a Broadway show tune and turned it into a slalom-like arrangement that was hard to negotiate. Above all trumpeter Gillespie and saxophonist Parker (a masterful blues player) made their propulsive, soaring solos the *raison d'être* of the song, though they also excelled on intimate, romantic themes.

But the speed of thought among jazz artists in the mid-1940s led to myriad other developments. The infusion of Afro-Cuban rhythms into bebop spawned Latin jazz, which had an emphasis on percussion instruments such as congas, bongos and timbales. Rhythm & blues was born when bluesy, highly rhythmic 'boogie-woogie' piano lines blended with short, snappy horn riffs, sometimes with raucous vocals, creating an irresistible dance style that was a major precursor to rock & roll.

Unparalleled creativity permeated 'modern jazz' between the 1950s and 1960s.[10] Musicians broadened their knowledge of harmony, painted marvellous chromatic colour in melody, essayed uncommon meters, blended softer, lighter rhythms and classical timbres in 'cool jazz'. They found liberation from the steeplechase of bebop chord changes in 'modal jazz' and expanded the existing vocabulary of their instruments.

The likes of Yusef Lateef, playing a double-reed horn from India, and Eric Dolphy, taking the bass clarinet from the classical world, would introduce 'other sounds.'

However, as jazz absorbed Brazilian bossa nova and Trinidadian calypso it continued to use foundational African-American music in the most fascinating way. The inflection of bebop towards gospel produced another new subgenre, called hard bop or soul jazz, and the blues remained a kind of core value to be used at will.

Remarkably the innovators had such strong personalities that they used the form as a springboard for *their thing*. Pianist Thelonious Monk's 'Blue Monk' makes such a playful, jaunty use of ascending semi-tones that the theme feels like an invitation to skip and smile at the same time. Trumpeter Miles Davis's 'All Blues' hovers and glides, his muted brass ethereal and sensual, creating the most subtle flicker of seduction. Saxophonist Wayne Shorter's 'Footprints' is a magnificent enigma, the melody unfolding briskly for two measures then resting for two like a burst of light before a shadow. His solo extends the emotional content by way of nuanced phrases – fluent, concise, raising and lowering energy, hinting, confirming, tantalizing – that push deeper into the sense of the unknown implied by the mesmeric atmosphere of the piece.

Each of the songs is a tried and tested twelve-bar blues but this is something that we are minded to forget, due to the wordless poetry flowing from the strength of character of the players and the precise conceptual choices. This is especially true of the six-beat meter of the Davis and Shorter tunes that have a mild time-stretch effect, a slow motion amid the progression of notes.

Shorter had a limitless, mischievous imagination and his restless creative energy shifted between astute points of view: 'When I improvise I guess I'm composing fast, and when I'm composing I'm improvising slowly.'[11]

In spite of this immense artistic achievement, African-Americans had to contend with the burden of 'colored only' facilities in public life, and the explicit signs relating to Jim Crow laws were compounded by implicit ones. A song could show how melodies sometimes flowed across the deeply racist terrain of the entertainment industry.

In 1957 the singer-pianist Nina Simone recorded a stupendous piece of music right on the cusp of jazz and R&B whose appeal lasts to this day: 'My Baby Just Cares For Me'. Joyous in its evocation of the trust between lovers, the lyric obliges Simone, who herself suffered for being a dark-skinned African-American woman, to compare herself to white ideals of female beauty, knowing that 'Lana Turner's smile' is the one thing she can never have. But if that seems jarring, the origin story of the song is utterly shocking.

It was originally performed by Eddie Cantor in blackface as part of the 1930 film *Whoopee!*, which reminds us that minstrel caricature of people of colour,

down to chalk white lips, burnt cork and bulging eyes, still existed in the early twentieth century.

Simone's version is a transformation because she injects a rich rhythmic energy into the arrangement courtesy of an unforgettable rolling piano riff, which, bridging the vocabularies of boogie-woogie and modern jazz, is a slow variation of the central motif of 'Bearcat Shuffle' by the pianist Mary Lou Williams, another

brilliant Black woman who emerged in the swing era but had a major influence on bebop players.

If the two songs were mixed to make 'My Bearcat Just Cares For Me', the spirit of two Black jazz icons, who had both rhythm and the blues, would come together explicitly. Simone's performance, complete with a brief, bracing piano solo, has such self-possession and charm she makes this tune from a dark place a light under a bushel.

BLACK RHYTHM ENERGY BLUES

It's hard to imagine that Simone was not aware of the racist cinematic context of 'My Baby Just Cares For Me', but she would have needed no additional motivation to write historic protest anthems such as

1964's 'Mississippi Goddam'. Her heroes had shown her the way, with Billie Holiday, Charles Mingus and Duke Ellington all making music that denounced the second-class citizenship of 'colored folk' in America.

The blues in jazz meant deeds as well as words. The blues in jazz meant truths.

Max Roach's *We Insist! Freedom Now Suite* was another civil rights-era musical landmark insofar as it linked the persecution of Black people in America with Black people in apartheid South Africa and urgently demanded equality in all societies. The music had memorable songs and startling passages of improvisation, notably vocalist Abbey Lincoln screaming to evoke rage at the great horror of racial violence, and the freedom demanded in the album's title vividly parallels a freedom in sound.

The political context for this creative decision was hugely important, but the idea of jazz artists exercising a degree of liberation from preset structures had been essayed by others, from Lennie Tristano and Dave Brubeck to Joe Harriott and Ornette Coleman, whose album *The Shape of Jazz to Come* was a notable entry in another subgenre that would eventually become known as 'free jazz', 'new thing' or avant-garde.

Some exponents pushed the envelope on the nature of sound, which could now be torrid if not violent, sometimes with shrieks and screams that were as disturbing as they were exhilarating. Albert Ayler, a saxophonist who emerged as a figurehead of the movement, had such an explosive tone that those who saw him live claimed that when he really hit the high notes, 'it was like a bomb going off.' Some critics condemned what they heard as 'anti-jazz'.

John Coltrane, the premier soloist of his generation, who made the spiritual masterpiece *A Love Supreme* in 1964, embraced the new direction. The echoes of very early blues and African-American sacred music in Coltrane's and Ayler's work gave them a particular appeal to activists such as the poet and playwright LeRoi Jones (later Amiri Baraka), who were seeking to develop an aesthetic that would be a true expression of African-American identity rather than a version

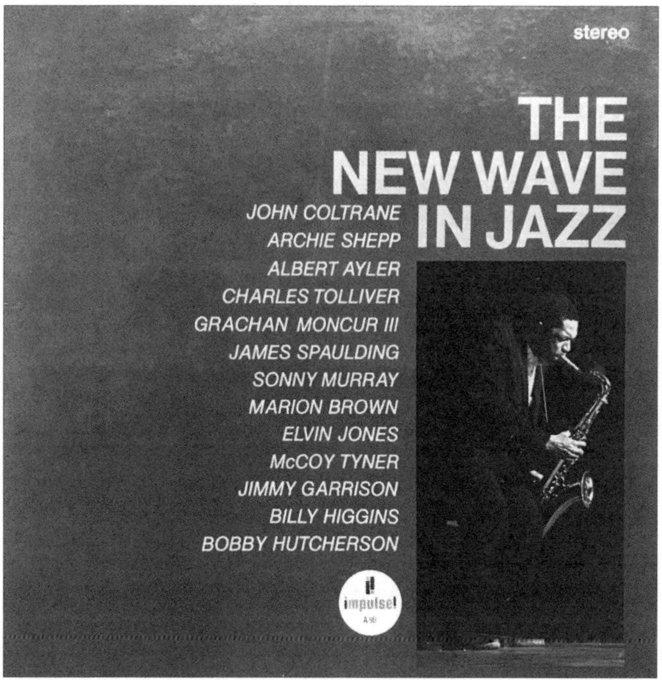

that was filtered for mass consumption. In 1965 the Black Arts Repertory Theatre, founded following the assassination of Malcolm X, held a benefit concert to that end at the Village Gate in New York that featured Coltrane, Ayler and Archie Shepp, among others. In the sleeve notes of the album of that performance, *The New Wave in Jazz*, Jones stated that the artists had socio-political and cultural value. 'The people who make the music are intellectuals or mystics or both. The black rhythm energy blues feeling (sensibility) is projected into the area of reflection.' Here the blues was as much life force as music, or rather, as Jones argued, a space for inquiry and discussion.

At roughly the same time there was concrete action taken to break free of the oppressive strictures of the music industry. The birth of artist-run labels and co-operative bodies such as the Jazz Composers Guild in New York, Black Artists Group in St. Louis (BAG) and The Association for the Advancement of Creative Musicians (AACM) in Chicago was a brave step towards independence, if not freedom.

A plethora of fine composers issued from the above, such as Bill Dixon, Julius Hemphill, Wadada Leo Smith, Muhal Richard Abrams and Anthony Braxton.

These were adventurous musicians who significantly broadened structural possibilities in jazz, sometimes pushing it to new levels of turbulent intensity, making it a 'hard blues', sometimes creating beguiling textures by way of advanced experiments with tonality. Though it was interesting that jazz was also increasingly impacted by non-Western rhythms and timbres. The sounds of

Africa and above all India would inspire musicians such as Alice Coltrane, also an adept of Hindu philosophy, and Don Cherry. They came to define themselves as universal artists, ready to embrace tanpura drones as much as gospel melodies as a framework for expressive, ecstatic improvisation.

Collaborating with German, British, Brazilian, Turkish or Swedish musicians – Stockholm would become his home – Cherry epitomized the global citizen of sound.

CRYSTALIZED

The relative commercial decline of jazz in the 1960s due to the rise of rock, soul and funk – the latter with its fizzing, syncopated drumming and hard-hitting, aggressive horns grown from the fertile soil of rhythm & blues – gave jazz musicians new sounds to consider. Drummer Tony Williams, guitarist John McLaughlin and trumpeter Miles Davis, all inspired by rock innovator Jimi Hendrix, saw the artistic value of 'plugging in' and embracing electric keyboards, Fender bass and wah-wah pedals to distort notes. Jazz-rock may have been an obvious term for their music, which had improvisation, heavy backbeats and power chords, but Davis spoke simply of 'directions in music'. The result was controversial, but the brooding atmospheres and murky low end of Davis's music – also spurred by an interest in urban Black youth culture – was historic.

As the divide widened between electric and acoustic in jazz there was a blurring of lines that said much about the way past and present could entwine in the music. Not all the instruments used since the heyday of swing and bebop were swiftly abandoned.

Indeed the combination of keyboard and double bass, which had been ushered in by Joe Zawinul and Victor Gaskin (in Cannonball Adderley's band), and developed by those such as Herbie Hancock, Chick Corea and Dave Holland (in Davis's band) and Lonnie Liston Smith and Cecil McBee, created an electro-acoustic lexicon that was an engrossing bridge between two sound worlds. One of which may have been perceived of at least synthetic, if not impure; the other organic, and pure. Yet together all these timbres upheld a key principle of creative music, which was to investigate whatever devices were available to stimulate players and listeners alike. Smith, whose pulsating song 'Expansions' was aglow with electronic textures and thickened by an 'unplugged', dense low register, explains the prevalent mindset.

The thing to understand is that in the 1970s we were all looking for new sounds and trying to get more sound from all of our instruments. Saxophone players like Pharoah Sanders were blowing so much that they didn't need an amp... he was the amp. And I saw the Fender Rhodes as a whole rainbow or a forest of colours, and the double bass was the big, tall tree in the middle of it, so everything came together with them. Yes, to say that we were actually on a kind of electro-acoustic thing is right.[12]

As a rejoinder to that statement one might also add that one of the most distinctive electric sounds of the decade – the beautifully round, thick tone of innovative fretless bass guitarist Jaco Pastorius – was borne of his desire to imitate the glissando of an acoustic bass, hence a new amplified noise carried with it an unamplified old one.

In any case acoustic music was still enriched by several visionary personalities.

Fifty years after the invigorations of ragtime and stride, Cecil Taylor hyper-adrenalized rhythm and Keith Jarrett slanted melody towards folk and classical in vastly different approaches to improvised solo piano that attracted different audiences. As for Herbie Hancock, who essayed every analog synthesizer made and fashioned futuristic afro-techno on albums such as *Sextant*, he still unplugged and played unaccompanied on occasion.

And if they were great orchestras of one there were great orchestras of many. The 1970s was a notable era for big bands. Gil Evans recast the psychedelic rock of Jimi Hendrix in a tonal world where French horns and clarinets met congas and guitars. Centipede, a fifty-piece combo led by British pianist Keith Tippett, built an audacious, voluminous bridge between the UK avant-garde and progressive rock scenes. Pianist Carla Bley brought a theatrical, often Weill-like quality to her all-action arrangements. And saxophonist-flautist Sam Rivers, who led a thirteen-piece unit on the astonishing album *Crystals*, made music of a frenetic, focused, elastic nature, moving from funky riffs to hard swing to tender interludes to exuberant fanfares, with the witheringly high pitches of the horns sometimes distorting as if they were a polyphonic synthesizer.

Rivers often superimposed rhythms and harmonies so extensively he managed to super-size his sound, creating what he called a 'dense constantly changing mass'. That could be an appropriate description for the electric music of Miles Davis.

At the end of the decade Archie Shepp led a thirty-piece orchestra that comprised brass, reeds, strings, acoustic and electric bass, piano, synthesizer, guitar and vocals on a repertoire that provided an unofficial summation of the history of African-American music, from gospel and blues to swing, funk, jazz-rock and avant-garde. The resulting sound was exhilarating. And its political charge was strong. The presence of Irene Datcher, Terry Jenoure and Akua Dixon – Black women musicians with braids and Afros – was a vivid reminder of the confluence of jazz, feminist sensibilities and civil rights movements reaching back to the 1950s. The name of the orchestra, the Attica Blues Big Band, highlighted an infamous case of institutional racism in America: the riot at Attica prison in New York. It

concerned the ghastly, inhumane conditions endured by mostly Black and Latino inmates and resulted in the deaths of forty-three men.

TRENDING

Remembered for the advance of technology in popular music, above all the rise of drum machines and synthesizers with greater possibilities for programming and sequencing, the 1980s was the first decade in the history of jazz in which there was no major new school or subgenre. While this state of affairs may have fuelled the argument that the music was moribund, it also meant that concepts were really at a premium, and that artists who thought clearly about how they wanted to express a particular vision of the world as well as their own character might see the absence of another 'movement' as an opportunity not a drawback. They led rather than followed.

Looking at an ages-old model such as the big band and seeing it not as a vehicle for pre-written composition but as a springboard for spontaneous composition was the brainchild of Lawrence D. 'Butch' Morris. He devised 'conduction', or 'an improvised duet for ensemble and conductor', discarding the sacrosanct principle of a score for orchestra. More to the point he was deliberately exercising his intellect, noting, revealingly, that the premise of his work was enquiry rather than certainty: 'The inception of creativity comes from the idea, and from the idea come questions. How you arrive at the answers to these questions (and the questions)...

will determine how you approach your art.'[13] As can be heard in a 1985 concert at The Kitchen in New York, Morris's music was full of structural whimsy that made it like a dark, disquieting, enticing opera, fragmenting as much as flowing, with stark shifts of tonality and texture executed by a band that featured talents such as harpist Zeena Parkins, guitarist Brandon Ross and alto saxophonist John Zorn (who would later become a prolific, highly eclectic composer and develop 'radical Jewish culture').

But the decade saw a huge paradigm shift in Black popular music as hip-hop made the art of rapping over scratches and beats a new modus operandi. The controversy over the threat this posed to the *real* band was intense, and while some jazz musicians decried it, others saw the sonic and narrative value of the new form. Max Roach collaborated with rappers, and Morris and Herbie Hancock both used turntables in their music, the latter achieving chart success on the mechanically funky, dance-oriented 'Rockit.'

If that hit said something about Hancock's genuine interest in pop culture and electronics, which had been present since the 1960s, important new artists made excellent music that also told the world who they were. They revealed identity. Steve Coleman manifested his interest in James Brown's funk, Charlie Parker's bebop, uncommon meters, ancient Black civilization and modern information technology. Courtney Pine explored his roots in reggae and Black British soul, and love of John Coltrane. Geri Allen embraced bebop, avant-garde and African music; Bobby McFerrin immersed himself in the tunefulness of The Beatles and Jimi Hendrix and the lyricism of Miles Davis. Wynton Marsalis demonstrated his allegiance to swing, blues, European classical music, African-American sociopolitical history and the lyricism of Miles Davis. Pat Metheny reflected his reverence for guitar heroes Wes Montgomery and Jim Hall, and his gift for improvisation and composition, which drew on folk, pop, Brazilian and ambient music.

While electric and acoustic schools benefitted from the presence of such strong personalities, jazz stayed political. Davis's *Tutu* and *Amandla* were strong anti-apartheid statements. Coleman's *Sine Die* could be a barbed comment on the ongoing deterioration of life chances for Black people under Ronald Reagan, particularly as the album sleeve shows the artist next to the warrior graffiti 'Death to Crack Dealers.'

Marsalis's *Black Codes (From the Underground)* celebrated the immense heroism of abolitionists and civil rights campaigners, calling for a liberation from 'the bondage of ignorance'[14] and higher standards in public education. Lawrence D. 'Butch' Morris made a blunt and unequivocal condemnation of the land of the free and home of the brave in *Current Trends in Racism in Modern America (A Work in Progress)*.

HOME COOKING

If discrimination continued to progress in the United States in the 1990s, Europe offered a haven of sorts in the mindset of many African-American artists, as it had done since the 1920s. And the Old World boasted countless talented players, with the scenes in France, Germany, Italy, Holland, Poland and Scandinavia all being dynamic. Norway had produced an international star in saxophonist Jan Garbarek, who brilliantly infused his work with the beauty of local folk idioms, but several of his compatriots also came to the fore, none more so than vocalist Sidsel Endresen.

In 1994 she made the beautiful album *Exile* featuring her compatriots trumpeter Nils Petter Molvær and keyboardist Jens Bugge Wesseltoft, and British pianist Django Bates. This was music of subtle detachment, Endresen often moving between spoken word and melodic phrases, and daringly leaving long pauses between some of her lines on songs that used classically inflected harmony to mesmerizing effect. She sang in English with a strikingly stark, limpid Nordic accent, which only increased her bold cultural authenticity. Endresen was nothing other than herself.

At roughly the same time another fine vocalist was asserting her originality with an altogether different concept. Active since the mid 1980s, Cassandra Wilson hit a major creative peak as a thinker and improviser by making the familiar unfamiliar.

The blues returned. But the setting was different. When Wilson investigated the classics of the canon, such as Robert Johnson's 'Come On in My Kitchen', she dispensed with drum kit, cymbals and piano, and used double bass, congas, guitar, mandolin and accordion to create a tonal world that was spare and spacious, every note thick and heavy as if baked in the heat of

her native Mississippi. Wilson took jazz back to one of its key foundations but created new sensations. Her arrangements, which often had strong Afro-Brazilian and Caribbean resonances, were hugely important. But first and foremost she proved that she had a profound understanding of the unavoidable conundrum the blues posed as well as the liberation it offered.

'I think a lot of jazz musicians are afraid of the blues because there's a certain emotional vulnerability when you get into this material,' she said. 'It's so bare you have to really be inventive.'[15] Sidsel Endresen certainly

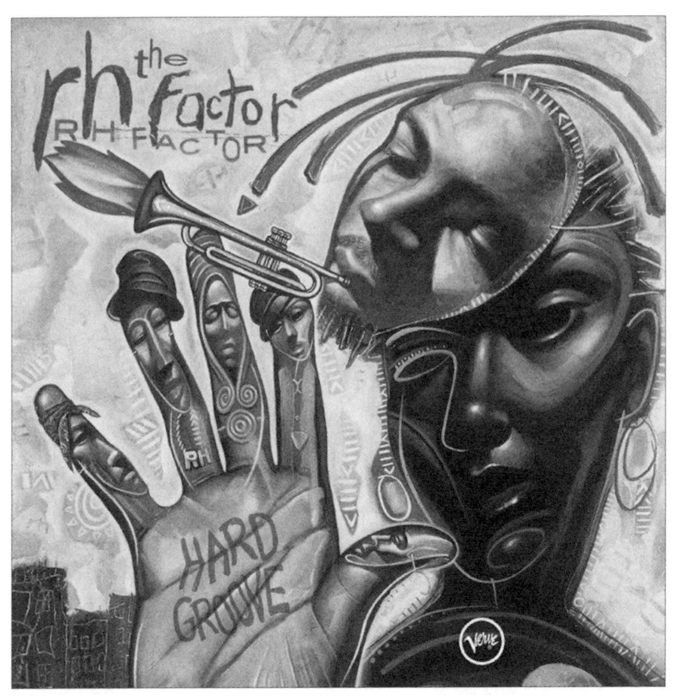

was. She later recorded a superb version of the soulful blues 'Tryin' Times', a song with a timeless sociopolitical message on man's inhumanity to man, in a style very much her own.

The blues remained instructive to players as well as singers in the 2000s and beyond. One could think of many ensembles that applied the form among myriad other vocabularies, but the piano trios of Geri Allen, Jason Moran, The Bad Plus and Robert Glasper showed how relevant and contemporary it remained to their imaginative eclecticism, which saw them draw on gospel, avant-garde, Japanese soundtracks, funk and rock to create music that was both steeped in history and highly contemporary.

But what was also important was the direct engagement of jazz artists with pop culture. Glasper would become a star for his skilful incorporation of soul and hip-hop with his band Experiment, but it was his former bandleader, the gifted trumpeter Roy Hargrove, who had shown the way with his electric group the RH Factor. After recording the fine album *Hard Groove* that featured the singers D'Angelo and Erykah Badu and rappers Common and Q-Tip, Hargrove made a thought-provoking statement about his approach 'The thing about being a jazz musician working with rappers is that you really should not come off superior. I don't think I'm better just because I can play a B-flat minor whatever. I learn from somebody who hears things *differently* to the way I do.'[16] Whether jazz has a philosophy of acceptance or non-judgemental thinking depends on the individual, given that there can be judgemental attitudes within jazz, as within all art forms. But Hargrove's philosophy of jazz was to open his mind as well as his ears, to listen, learn and move, from acoustic bebop to electric funk and hop-hop via Afro-Cuban rhythms and orchestral ballads. He switched on and off to technology as he saw fit. He was a part of changing traditions and a tradition of change.

CHAPTER THREE

NOW AND THEN, AND THEN AND NOW

TWO DUOS WHO DANCE IN SOUND

Pianist Muhal Richard Abrams, long-standing president of the Chicago-based Association for the Advancement of Creative Musicians (AACM) – a body that produced significant composers such as saxophonist Roscoe Mitchell (one of the first members of the organization) of the group Art Ensemble of Chicago – performed two improvised duets in New York between 2009 and 2010. The first with tenor saxophonist Fred Anderson, the second with George Lewis on trombone and laptop. The music was later issued on the double CD *SoundDance*.

Together both sets provided a fitting summary of the talents of veteran players who did not lack vitality. Abrams, 79 years old at the time, had been recording since the late 1960s and had amassed a discography that included fine solo piano, small group and big band works. The first set with Anderson (who was 80 years old), was a bravura display of intuitive creation as the pair moved seamlessly between streaming percussive energy and graceful tranquillity, in which advanced listening skills and reflexive decision-making came into play. The second set, with Lewis, then 58 years old, and a pioneer of computer-based music since the late 1970s, was a beguiling musical adventure in which the horn and piano flurried and floated over electronic textures that vividly evoked primeval rural spaces as well as the stark, unsettling noise of urban environments.

The same man playing a brass instrument that had been used in jazz since the early twentieth century and deploying digital equipment from the twenty-first so creatively was a powerful symbol of the way past and present can often elide in improvised music.

What was especially interesting was the fact that a laptop was not even perceived as an instrument at all by some, let alone a jazz instrument. A deep suspicion and prejudice existed among many players and listeners who did not consider such a device to be legitimate, echoing views on the turntables and drum machines that had replaced 'real' musicians in hip-hop. Tellingly, Abrams stated that his earliest flirtations with synthesizers were done almost in secret because of the stigma around a *fake* device that lacked the purity of an acoustic piano, which was seen as a sacrosanct object. Fourteen years after *SoundDance*, the sight of a laptop in a jazz group is so widespread it is no longer shocking, and the idea of cutting-edge technology not only adding interesting effects to improvised music but being used as a means of improvisation is a norm.

The electro-acoustic ensembles of Evan Parker, a titan of the British avant-garde, and the interesting collaborations between sound artist Ikue Mori and several jazz musicians bear this out. But the work of any number of pianists, guitarists, singers, drummers and horn players inspired by Eddie Harris – who used an electric saxophone, octave dividers and echoplex back in the 1960s – is also part of this culture.

In fact, the whole point is that this embrace of technology can produce something indefinable that is beholden to the guiding principle in jazz of pushing towards what has not been heard before, of making possible the seemingly impossible. Hearing guitarist

Mary Halvorson for the first time was a shock, because she was using a pedal board that seemed to make some of her notes run backwards. Others seemed to mimic science fiction ray guns. Then again, another excellent guitarist, the Beninois Lionel Loueke, has achieved similar feats with both digital processing and also by placing strips of paper under his strings, turning his instrument into a kind of buzzing balaphone. His lo-fi accessories do not sound any less rich than his hi-fi.

Technology ends up being a vague term. A piece of carved wood a musician holds to their chest may have been invented centuries before a slim tray of circuitry encased in plastic and metal, but it is not necessarily older if the sound drawn from it stimulates.

Ultimately, jazz artists use resources from different points in time according to what serves their specific vision. There are fewer clarinet and cornet players active today than there are saxophonists, but the former instruments do not sound at all passé when they are deployed by composers and improvisers who have a degree of imagination.

Ironically, old instruments can be new in certain circumstances. The key factor is the culture of the audience, as confirmed by this telling anecdote from Neal Evans of Soulive, a 2000s band modelled on the classic organ trio led by the likes of Jimmy Smith in the 1950s. 'One of the things that struck me when we met young black guys into hip-hop is how fascinated they were with our set-up. I mean we're playing in front of some kids who have *never* seen a Hammond organ before. You imagine that? An integral part of jazz history came to them for the first time. They just hadn't seen this kind of keyboard before.'[17] However, many *had* already heard it: on vinyl.

ALL POINTS EAST

The use of loops of records by jazz artists on the Blue Note label, recorded mostly in the 1960s and 1970s, changed the sound of hip-hop. DJs started to dig the organ of Dr Lonnie Smith, the guitar of Grant Green, the saxophone of Lou Donaldson, the drums of Idris Muhammad, and the keyboards of the Mizell Brothers (who produced albums for Donald Byrd and Bobbi Humphrey, among others). These were nuggets.

In the 1990s the jazz sample, or 'Blue breakbeat' in reference to Blue Note, acquired kudos because all of the aforementioned sounds gave listeners and dancers a form of sonic stimulus that was different to the 1980s hip-hop dominated by James Brown beats.

If clubgoers were exposed to jazz via rap records, then so too was a generation of young jazz musicians. While formally studying Duke Ellington, Miles Davis and John Coltrane they had their heads turned by A Tribe Called Quest's 'Electric Relaxation' because of the ethereal drift of Ronnie Foster's 'Mystic Brew', on which the song is built. Aspiring players thirsty for knowledge of a demanding, stimulating art form heard fragments of it filtered through popular music in which the manipulation of audio captured on a piece of vinyl rather than the command of an instrument is king. Essentially that meant the discovery had a dramatic

change of context because the organ, guitar, horn and drum breaks were accompanied by the flow of original rhymes that added new rhythm to all these historic sounds. Furthermore, the original instruments usually had a shift of pitch, panning or filter effects that altered their nature. There was notable abstraction, redirection and re-contextualization as a result. In fact, there is a generation of jazz musicians who are indebted to the archival research role played by hip-hop DJs and producers because it has brought to light previously hidden and neglected artists. Hunting for beats, the proverbial 'crate digging', has helped to construct an alternative history of jazz, a counter-narrative, that largely celebrates jazz musicians who ran their own labels, had limited distribution and media exposure, and were generally footnotes in academic studies of the music – if they were there at all. There were countless musicians who had simply slipped under the radar.

This turn of events reflects the complex relationship between Black pop and art music, or how the two strands have been mutually beneficial through the use of technology and significant structural change. Hip-hop was enriched by the sounds of jazz, and also became a database for 'lost' jazz. A new genre taught an old one about itself. DJs and record collectors helped to shine a light on 1970s labels such as Tribe, Black Jazz and Black Fire – all trailblazing, independent operations that issued music by Phil Ranelin, Wendell Harrison and Oneness of Juju. They all built on the modernism of the 1960s by frequently incorporating complex African rhythms, funky licks, strong vocal chants, interesting harmony and a bold political message into their work.

Then there was Strata-East Records, co-founded by trumpeter Charles Tolliver and pianist Stanley Cowell, both excellent composers who had played with Max Roach, among others. They created one of the most impressive catalogues of independent jazz in the 1970s and early 1980s by recording a wide range of musicians who plotted an interesting personal path through blues, swing, modal and avant-garde styles.

Albums by the aforesaid Tolliver and Cowell as well as by Clifford Jordan, Charles Brackeen, John Hicks,

Charles Rouse and Pharoah Sanders were instrumental in keeping alive the spirits of pioneers such as Thelonious Monk and John Coltrane, among others, sometimes by creating dense orchestral sounds in a band that featured two drummers, two double basses, tuba, horns, vocals and many layers of percussion.

Also important is the Nimbus West label that released music by, among others, Horace Tapscott. His collective Union of God's Musicians and Artists Ascension (UGMAA) was a vital resource to the Black creative community of Los Angeles. And the doyen of independent jazz Sun Ra, whose Arkestra, founded in the 1950s, is still playing his cosmic, Afro-centric songs today, over three decades after his passing.

Discovering such music in the 1990s and 2000s was exhilarating for those of us whose knowledge of jazz was largely restricted to the standard 'hall of fame', because it filled in major blanks in history and excitingly intersected with the hip-hop culture that had also shaped hearts and minds – and moved feet – at the same time.

Winter in America was a fine album recorded for Strata-East by the ingenious political poet-proto-rapper Gil Scott-Heron with pianist-flautist Brian Jackson. The album cemented the idea that jazz – the past of Black music – was inextricably linked to its present – hip-hop – and it was the use of another of the label's songs in one of the bona fide anthems of the latter genre that built a vital chronological and cultural continuum.

'One Love' by Nas was produced by Q-Tip and featured a sample of the Heath Brothers's 'Smilin' Billy

Suite Part II', a tune with a dream-state finesse due to its blend of double bass, piano and kalimba (an African finger harp), played by Stanley Cowell. It sounded like a keyboard that bridged the digital age and ancient times.

The beauty of all these timbres sent an explicit message to future beat-makers about the benefit of tracking down the more obscure recordings in jazz. It was also a kind of unofficial historical guide for jazz musicians who had much to gain not just by studying the looped fraction of a song, but by also further researching its creators.

RHYTHM TO RHYTHM-A-NING

Given the greater access to the work of known and unknown figures from the past that exists in the internet age, it is no surprise that reinterpretations have proliferated. Musicians all over the world, but especially in West Africa, reprise the music of jazz-rock heroes Weather Report and bass guitar innovator Jaco Pastorius (mentioned earlier), whose finely wrought, often funky, pulsating compositions have also been arranged for big bands.

The British-European group دمحأ [Ahmed], comprises pianist Pat Thomas, saxophonist Seymour Wright, double bassist Joel Grip and drummer Antonin Gerbal. They have been fearlessly imaginative in their interpretation of the songs of Ahmed Abdul-Malik, the Sudanese-American double bassist-oud player who brought strong African and Arabic flavours to jazz by turning his originals into epic new songs that surf torrid, giant waves of rhythm and fluctuating harmonies that build to intense climaxes. But the music of one of Abdul-Malik's bandleaders, Thelonious Monk – a great composer – has also been played by dozens of musicians in America, Europe and beyond, some notable examples being British saxophonists Xhosa Cole and Tony Kofi. One could also mention two very different pianists, the Panamanian Danilo Pérez and the American Jason Moran. All of the above have infused new timbres and rhythms to tunes like 'Rhythm-a-Ning.'

A kind of time-stretching historical chain forms as a result. It's not just that a song is passed on through the ages, but more that the adaptation can give insights on the original melody and rhythm, as well as the personality of the new performer and 'old' composer. So, Moran playing Monk says something about the way Moran hears drums in the age of hip-hop and how Monk heard drums in the age of bebop.

A GODDAM COUP D'ETAT

Then became now in the most uncanny way in January 2025. Singer Ni Maxine proved that there is a real

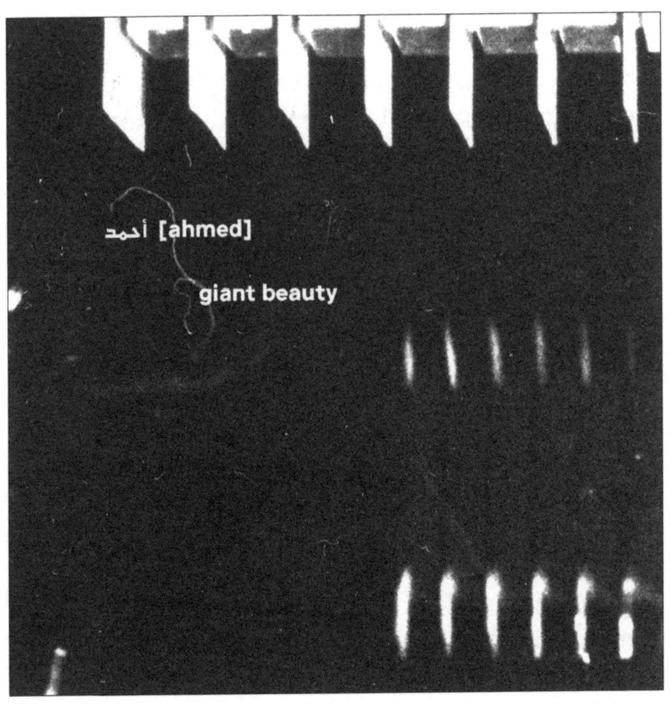

tightrope to walk every time an improvising musician is on stage. When a verse of Nina Simone's 'Four Women' slipped Maxine's mind, an artful, wordless vocal left her mouth, triggered by creative reflexes that echoed those of vocal icon Ella Fitzgerald, who famously salvaged the standard 'Mack the Knife' when she had to improvise after forgetting the lyrics at a concert in Berlin in 1960.

Maxine's passing fall and rise added a sharp edge to the timeless tale of Black female solidarity for 'Four Women', because the singers standing next to her – Laura Mvula, Corinne Bailey-Rae and China Moses –

willed her on to triumph. As did a fully engaged crowd. The concert was a celebration of Simone, the pianist, singer and activist who masterfully interpreted anything from jazz and R&B to pop and folk. It was presented by Nu Civilisation Orchestra, a band with residency at the South Bank Centre in London. It was conducted by Peter Edwards and featured several fine players in its ranks, including saxophonist Denys Baptiste, flautist Rowland Sutherland and pianist Sarah Tandy to name but a few. The ensemble was augmented further by a large, lush string section.

Simone had a vast repertoire, but the set list was astutely chosen and featured classic songs such as 'Little Girl Blue', 'Feeling Good', 'African Mailman' and 'Sinner Man'. They all drew hearty applause for the interpretation of beautiful melodies, variously drawn from Broadway show tunes and gospel traditions, but the most electrifying moment of the evening came when China Moses, the daughter of the legendary singer Dee Dee Bridgewater, reprised the civil rights anthem 'Mississippi Goddam'.

Moses had a visceral, bluesy holler, which conveyed the righteous defiance that fuelled many of Simone's greatest works and, in a moment of expertly handled drama, she appeared to inhabit the thought that Alabama had her 'so upset', making it clear she was ready to fight for equality. The energy resonated strongly on the song that had been summarily banned by US radio stations over sixty years before the concert.

Earlier in January the Belgian capital Brussels hosted its annual jazz festival. One of the highlights of the nine-day event was the appearance, in the venue Flagey, of Irreversible Entanglements. The quintet, from the USA, featured strong instrumentalists (bassist Luke Stewart, drummer Tcheser Holmes, trumpeter Aquiles Navarro, saxophonist Keir Neuringer) combined with the charismatic, thought-provoking poet Camae Ayewa, aka Moor Mother. The band created torridly circular rhythms that shifted incrementally as she varied the form and content of her delivery, sometimes slowing down to single staccato beats, sometimes quickening to fluid speech. The band's masterstroke was a dramatic swerve in the second half of the set to a pure percussion barrage, in which congas, bells, rattles and shakers unleashed an earthy Afro-Brazilian vibration that pushed against the formality of a seated audience who accepted an invitation to dance.

As Irreversible Entanglements exited the stage to thunderous applause, Stewart took to the mike and shouted 'remember Patrice Lumumba!' Nothing could have been more appropriate, given that he was referring to the leader of the Democratic Republic of the Congo who was assassinated by local rivals with the complicity of the outgoing Belgian colonial government, the rapacious mining industry and the CIA, on the same date as the Flagey concert, 17 January, but in 1961. It is an anniversary of modern-day infamy.

An injustice perpetrated decades ago is deeply pertinent given that the Congo is still riven by internal strife and targeted by multinational industrialists who lust for its precious minerals that power the iPhones held up to film Irreversible Entanglements.

With great serendipity, the first half of the Brussels jazz festival featured a screening of *Soundtrack to a Coup D'Etat*, the remarkable 2024 documentary made by Johan Grimonprez about Lumumba and the fervent responses to Africa's plight by African and Black American musicians. Appearing in the movie, alongside Max Roach, Abbey Lincoln, Franco and Miriam Makeba, is Nina Simone. At his concert on the closing weekend of the event, British pianist Ashley Henry reprised 'Mississippi Goddam'. It had an entirely different harmony and rhythm to the Nu Civilization Orchestra's London rendition.

SOUND
TRACK to a
d' COUP
ETAT
WINNER
sundance
a JOHAN GRIMONPREZ film
filmswelike

KEEP ON MOVING

There was something life enhancing about the sight of Simone briefly projected on to a big screen at the start of the Nu Civilisation Orchestra gig, as if she were keeping an eye on the audience, possibly ready to call us all to order in case the whim took her.

Additional visual stimulus to music can be powerful, and jazz as a multimedia art form has deep roots. Jazz artists have appeared on film since the 1920s, written dozens of soundtracks and collaborated with numerous writers and poets. Also fascinating are projects by jazz composers and choreographers such as Duke Ellington and Alvin Ailey in the 1960s and Max Roach and Bill T. Jones in the 1990s.

Although known as a minimalist experimental composer, Julius Eastman, who was active in the 1980s, also had a keen interest in choreography. It was notable to see British singer-movement artist Elaine Mitchener explore his work in a performance at the Barbican Centre in London in 2025. Backed by a three-piece ensemble – Neil Charles (double bass), Xhosa Cole (tenor sax, flute) and Jason Yarde (alto sax) – she presented an hour-long suite in which she pushed her voice and body into absorbing, at times punishing, moments of expression. It was full of anguish and ecstasy, primeval rumblings, operatic flights, soulful incantations, squalls of noise and a relentless chanted mantra: 'Stay on it. moving and grooving.' My neighbour – sighing and hissing with irritation – left before the halfway mark, but the point was that this was a whole rather than a collection of parts, and in the fabulous climactic moment of the piece a spare, barren electronic crackle morphed into a highly melodic dance tune that had all the charm of a swaying calypso. The release was joyous, both for the artist and audience, because we had entered a world where sound and movement were sufficiently fluid for a West Indian folk rhythm to blend with austere, abstract sounds.

Moving Eastman was a perfect summary of jazz as a multimedia expression that is wide-ranging in form and content. Double bassist Charles and saxophonist Yarde potently enhanced the acoustic timbres of their instruments with electronic effects drawn from samplers. This was given further depth by the haunting reverberations created by sound artist Michael Picknett, while the choreography and direction of Dam Van Huynh brought a sustained theatricality to the performance, as if Mitchener – whose vocal range runs from the burliest baritone to a soaring soprano – was fully inhabiting Eastman's spirit. This was intensely political work. All the lyrics she spoke or sang were quotes from a range of figures such as poet-singer Jeanne Lee, the feminist theorist known as bell hooks, sociologist Stuart Hall and jazz legend John Coltrane; it shed light on Black identity and humanity in the broadest sense. The most resonant line was from Eastman himself, who pledged to be 'Black to the fullest, a musician to the fullest, homosexual to the fullest.' There is no compromise on the self and the art.

Eastman also advocated 'the carin' and the sharin'', which could be seen as a message for community cohesion as well as cross-disciplinary practise to which

American saxophonist Immanuel Wilkins – who has impressed since his emergence in 2020 – might relate. He has collaborated with like-minded souls in the world of visual arts such as Kennedy Yanko, Leslie Hewitt, Cauleen Smith and Ja'Tovia Gary – their work ranges from sculpture to photography, video, film and exciting hybrids of all of the above. Wilkins sees a historical lineage into which this cross-fertilization fits.

I think about my favourite musicians who, back in the day, were close with other people in parallel traditions and creative universes. Painters were tight with musicians, writers, designers, visual artists, everybody was kind of intermingled. I feel like I have some kind of responsibility to bridge the gap because I do feel that things are cliquey. The music world is cliquey, the jazz world is cliquey, the art world is cliquey, the fashion world, the writing world... everything felt like you couldn't really break through and cross-pollinate. So I started to go and see artists that I really loved, I'd go just support their work, and then we would build relationships.[18]

One figure that has symbolized this in no uncertain terms is pianist and visual artist Jason Moran. Inspired as much by Austrian abstract expressionist painter Egon Schiele as he is by jazz great Duke Ellington, Moran is highly imaginative in his multimedia work. Notable examples include accompanying skateboarders while performing with his trio The Bandwagon, scoring music for the ballets of Alonzo

King, and using video art by David Dempewolf and conceptual art by Glenn Ligon in an interpretation of the 1959 Thelonious Monk Town Hall concert.

ANOTHER BOPPER

Multimedia activity is not the only link between Moran and Wilkins. The former was a one-time mentor to the latter, offering invaluable advice when the saxophonist was a new member of his band in 2017. 'Jason was a big help', Wilkins recalls. The older musician opened his mind: 'He took me on my first European tour in my sophomore year of college, and would just encourage me to get outside when we were on the road, to go check out some art, go for a walk and look at architecture.'[19]

If such words of wisdom possibly changed an artistic outlook then they were drawn from a place of conviction, for Moran has spoken at length of the lessons he himself learned from a range of older musicians such as Muhal Richard Abrams and Andrew Hill. Both men were important figures of the 1960s avant-garde who kept on making excellent music with small groups and big bands into the 2000s. Moreover, one of Hill's junior band members from the 1980s, saxophonist Greg Osby, later became a mentor to Moran. A continuum duly formed. Culture went from elder to younger.

Peer groups have always formed important bands in jazz, and it is essential that teenagers or older players who have grown together also have opportunities, but the aforesaid collaborations – mentorships – are a kind

of intergenerational exchange that has long existed in jazz, whereby experienced players helped less experienced ones with techniques, certainly prior to the development of formal jazz education.

Seeing Moran grow from the debut he made with Osby into the artist he is today has been exciting for the way the already strong character he showed at the early stage of his career has simply become more adventurous. But what is especially important is the continued impact on him of other older players in addition to the aforementioned.

Moran has worked with the late Sam Rivers, Charles Lloyd and Archie Shepp, three legendary saxophonists whose careers began in the 1960s and unfolded in interesting ways that saw them explore a wide range of musical styles and settings. The lessons Moran learned as a result, not just on rhythm, harmony and improvisation, but on the more abstract question of how to present and order a set list and bring the right pace to a performance so as to fully engage an audience, are invaluable to say the least.

Perhaps most importantly, the likes of Lloyd and Shepp – both in their 80s – are part of a 'golden generation' in jazz that will not last forever. The large number of their peers who have passed in the last few years, from Wayne Shorter and Ahmad Jamal to Martial Solal and Andy Bey, makes it clear that every moment they have left is precious – and not just because of their ongoing musical ability, which in Shepp's case is borne out by an astounding recent duet with Franco-Syrian flautist Naïssam Jalal.

These older musicians are storytellers in every sense. They construct narrative in sound but also enthral us in word and remind us of the value of lived experience, or – more to the point – that the giants of jazz are human beings with strong personalities.

Jazz needs its history for the simple reason that jazz history, like all history, is subject to investigation in order to gain the greatest understanding of how and by whom the history is made in the first place. The music comes from people who lived real lives. When the 82-year-old American saxophonist Billy

Harper appeared with his quartet at Ronnie Scott's in London in February 2025, he carried real gravitas to the stage, strikingly clad in a long black leather tunic he called a *shakeela*. This was a man who had made timeless, spiritually charged music in the 1970s and played with the giants of modern jazz (Max Roach, Art Blakey, Gil Evans). After he had regaled the audience at the sold-out event with songs such as 'Croquet Ballet' (a noble lament that floats on a lithe six-beat groove and on which he took a beautifully poised, yearning solo),[20] an unusual thing happened. Harper conducted an impromptu Q&A with the audience.

There was a question about one of the many bandleaders he worked with, trumpeter Lee Morgan. Harper grinned widely and chuckled 'Oh, he was a bopper, alright!' No sooner had the words passed his lips than he leaned forward in a slightly boxer-like pose. There was a double meaning at play. Bopper referred to the subgenre of 1950s hard bop, the generally slower, gospel-inflected outgrowth of 1940s bebop, but Harper also seemed to hint that there was something dynamic – if not combative – about Morgan. 'I mean you saw him boppin' down the street, he was always ready.' For what exactly? To solo at a jam session? To play the chord changes of any standard that was called? To bust a move on the dancefloor at a party? Or possibly to 'bop' his way out of trouble if ever confronted by the wrong company? Maybe all these things were true. The implication was that Morgan had energy.

In the space of a few moments, the richness of African-American colloquialism came emphatically to

bear on the formal setting of a concert. It was a privilege to hear the wry humour in Harper's voice amid his engaging stories and gestural communication.

He also revealed that he made his first appearance at Ronnie Scott's back in 1973 as a member of the Thad Jones/Mel Lewis Orchestra, a fabulous long-running big band that played in a wide range of styles. It was a part of Harper's formative years. Incredibly, there was somebody in the audience in 2025 who was actually at *that* gig. For a moment the idea of a punter with over fifty years' listening experience connecting with a musician with a commensurate amount of playing experience (and who had channelled countless concerts, recording sessions and thousands of hours of practise into accomplished composing and improvising that made his music a thing of beauty), became a metaphor for what jazz can be: a bond in the passage of time. What happened then is dancing with what is happening now. Listener and player are part of a shared memory, a nostalgia that resists erasure.

ALL MY TOMORROWS

In 2024, when Trinidadian trumpeter-composer Etienne Charles presented his Creole Orchestra at Soul Mama in London he was joined by a range of local players drawn from various sources rather than his original US band. In so doing he upheld an ongoing spirit of international collaboration in jazz. Over the years skilled composers, notably the Americans Gil Evans, George Russell and Sam Rivers, and the

Brazilian Hermeto Pascoal, have all led big bands comprising British musicians, but Charles's gig was particularly interesting because of its educational subtext. An associate professor of Jazz at the University of Miami, the 42-year-old has long worked with the Royal Academy of Music in London. Its head of jazz, 49-year-old Nick Smart, assembled the horn section while 24-year-old Luke Bacchus was on piano. He studied at Trinity Laban Conservatoire, which, along with RAM, Guildhall School of Music, Leeds College of Music and Birmingham Conservatoire, provides jazz courses taught by many leading players on the British scene. Artists such as Nikki Yeoh and Julian Joseph, both excellent pianists, prepare young people before they enrol at those institutions, as does National Youth Jazz Orchestra (NYJO).

What has made a major difference to the recent history of jazz education in Britain is the existence of development organisations such as Tomorrow's Warriors. It was founded by Gary Crosby – former member of the influential 1980s Black British big band Jazz Warriors – and Janine Irons. Both Crosby and Irons have valiantly stood on a platform of diversity, inclusion and gender balance, and have nurtured countless young players, several of whom – for example Soweto Kinch, Yazz Ahmed, Shabaka Hutchings, Nubya Garcia and Femi Koleoso[21] – have gone on to enjoy considerable success.

Another invaluable community-based music education initiative is Kinetika Bloco, whose tutors include South African trumpeter Claude Deppa,

British tuba player Andy Grappy and Trinidadian steel pan player Wade Austin, and which has built an interesting bridge between jazz, choreography and Caribbean carnival culture.

Such is the abundance of new players arriving everywhere in the world – not just in Britain – and facilitated by very high standards of training, it is ever more difficult to keep track of the development of jazz today in absolute terms. Artists have a habit of either releasing their music on independent labels or self-distribution, making it more or less impossible to give a one hundred per cent accurate assessment of the state of the music because there are significant works that slip under the radar. We have to constantly look back to find them. Yet emerging artists such as Kirke Kaja (Estonia), Mariá Portugal (Brazil)[22] and Christie Dashiell (USA) are proof positive of a continuum of talent in jazz. Dashiell is a fabulously gifted singer-composer who, since making her debut in 2016, has worked with Black Lives, the international collective founded in the wake of the Black Lives Matter movement. Her 2023 album *Journey in Black* is a fine collection of songs that highlight Dashiel's lyrical as well as melodic ability, and in 2025 she collaborated with drummer Terri Lyne Carrington on *We Insist 2025!*. It is a reimagining of Max Roach and Abbey Lincoln's 1960 civil rights-era masterpiece *We Insist! Freedom Now Suite* that underlines the ongoing desire of jazz artists to address modern social justice issues.

Indeed, Jason Moran argues 'jazz is the understory to everything.' And as one of the pianist's sources of inspiration, Thelonious Monk, showed so ingeniously, music can reveal the moving fine line between ugly and beauty.

Jazz is a young art form, but its rapid pace of change has produced many vocabularies that make it mature beyond its years, throwing tantalizingly into doubt our sense of a timeline and what might constitute past and present. Everything previously stated can be relevant to what is yet to be stated. This teasing back and forth, this alchemy of old begetting new, a composition of then informing one of now, is integral to the music, which

continues to straddle acoustic and electric worlds, responding to the advance of technology by embracing digital devices as and when it is considered appropriate. The ambiguity – the sense of mystery – that can be created when analogue and digital combine in an improvisatory context is a highly interesting aspect of contemporary jazz, though there is enormous beauty to be heard in a solo voice, guitar, piano or saxophone performance, as there is in the sound of a piano trio, saxophone quartet or big band. Or a big band featuring steel pan as well as keys, congas, brass and reeds.

While grown from African-American history, jazz is a universal music that invites exponents to uphold the spirit of its pioneers, all the while bringing something of themselves to the process, questing and questioning as much as asserting and answering. It can be a long and winding road as opposed to a straight and narrow one that occasionally leads to damning dissent and disapproval. Indeed the ingenuity of some of the now accepted legends was occasionally perceived as ineptitude when they were active, and if a ticket holder walks out of a concert in 2025, it is worth remembering that some improvising musicians were threatened with violence in 1965. Eccentricity, oddity and unorthodoxy as well as unstinting rigour, vast research and fearless imagination are all part of the intriguing DNA of jazz. We should embrace not one but all of the music's many traditions, which may possibly do justice to both its progenitors and successors, extraordinary individuals who also belong to creative communities. They run the gamut from the orchestra of one to the orchestra of many. They invite us to think, feel and dance;[23] they keep probing, pressing and pushing towards something new and something else. And when they have found the answer to a question, they move on to another question.

FURTHER READING

James Baldwin, 'Sonny's Blues' (*Partisan Review*, 1957)

Randall Grass, *Great Spirits: Portraits of Life-changing World Music Artists* (University Press of Mississippi, 2009)

W. C. Handy, *Father of the Blues: An Autobiography* (Macmillan, 1941)

Ajay Heble and Rob Wallace (eds), *People Get Ready: The Future of Jazz is Now!* (Duke University Press, 2014)

LeRoi Jones (Amiri Baraka), *Blues People: Negro Music in White America* (William Morrow, 1963)

Ashley Kahn, *The House That Trane Built: The Story of Impulse Records* (W. W. Norton, 2006)

Robin D. G. Kelley, *Africa Speaks, America Answers: Modern Jazz in Revolutionary Times* (Harvard University Press, 2012)

David Margolick, *Strange Fruit: Billie Holiday, Café Society and an Early Cry for Civil Rights* (Payback Press, 2000)

Tricia Rose, *Black Noise: Rap Music and Black Culture in Contemporary America* (Wesleyan University Press, 1994)

A. B. Spellman, *Four Lives in the Bebop Business* (Limelight, 1985)

Derrick Stewart-Baxter, *Ma Rainey and the Classic Blues Singers* (Stein & Day, 1970)

Mark Stryker, *Jazz From Detroit* (University of Michigan Press, 2019)

John F. Szwed, *Space is the Place: The Lives and Times of Sun Ra* (Payback Press, 1997)

Horace Tapscott (edited by Steven Isoardi), *Songs of the Unsung: The Musical and Social Journey of Horace Tapscott* (Duke University Press, 2001)

Valerie Wilmer, *As Serious As Your Life: Black Music and the Free Jazz Revolution, 1957–1977* (Allison & Busby, 1977)

FURTHER LISTENING

James P. Johnson, 'Carolina Shout' (Okeh, 1921)

Louis Armstrong, *Louis & The Blues Singers 1925–1929* (EMI, 1972)

Jimmie Lunceford, *For Dancers Only* (Decca, 1949)

Jimmy Giuffre, *Free Fall* (Columbia, 1963)

Eric Dolphy, *Out to Lunch!* (Blue Note, 1964)

Marion Brown, *Afternoon of a Georgia Faun* (ECM, 1970)

Frank Foster featuring Dee Dee Bridgewater, *The Loud Minority* (Mainstream, 1972)

Hermeto Pascoal, *Slaves Mass* (Warner, 1977)

Louis Moholo Octet, *Spirits Rejoice!* (Ogun, 1978)

Henri Texier, *A Cordes et à Cris* (JMS, 1979)

Betty Carter, *The Audience With Betty Carter* (Bet-Car, 1980)

New Air featuring Cassandra Wilson, *Air Show No. 1* (Black Saint, 1986)

Irene Schweizer/Andrew Cyrille, *Irene Schweizer/Andrew Cyrille* (Intakt, 1989)

Dianne Reeves, *Art and Survival* (EMI, 1994)

Jayne Cortez & The Firespitters, *Taking the Blues Back Home* (Harmolodic, 1996)

William Parker featuring Leena Conquest, *Raining on the Moon* (Thirsty Ear, 2002)

Robert Mitchell's Panacea, *Trust* (F-IRE, 2004)

Craig Taborn, *Avenging Angel* (ECM, 2011)

Fay Victor & Herbie Nichols SUNG, *Life Is Funny That Way* (Tao Forms, 2024)

LIST OF ILLUSTRATIONS

ENDNOTES

1. Interview with author, New York, 1998.
2. 'The Big Band Theory', *The Guardian*, 2 January 2024.
3. *Ibid.*
4. Interview with the author, October 2023.
5. The artists are omitted to highlight the importance of the songs, several of which have been covered. The composers are: 'Body and Soul' (Green/Heyman/Sour/Eyton, 1930), 'Acknowledgement' (John Coltrane, 1965), 'Beatrice' (Sam Rivers, 1965), 'Tell Me' (Donald Byrd/Larry Mizell, 1976), 'Just the Two of Us' (Bill Withers/William Salter/Ralph MacDonald, 1980), 'You Move Me' (Cassandra Wilson, 1997), 'All Matter' (Bilal, 2010), 'Three Gifts (From a Nigerian Mother to God)' (Anthony Branker, 2024), 'Black Iris' (Nnenna Freelon/Alan Pasqua 2025).
6. 'Some People Don't Think It's a Serious Instrument', *The Guardian*, 24 February 2023.
7. Interview with the author, 2005.
8. Sleeve notes of Jelly Roll Morton, *Jelly Roll Morton 1923/24* (Milestone, 1974).
9. '(What Did I Do to be So) Black And Blue' composed by Fats Waller, Harry Brooks and Andy Razaf in 1929.
10. Modern jazz in the 1950s and 1960s is such a vast subject that there is not sufficient space for in-depth study here. Art Blakey, Freddie Hubbard, Lee Morgan, Sonny Rollins, Charles Mingus, Bill Evans, Jackie McLean and Randy Weston are just a few of the leading American artists. Europeans include René Urteger, Barney Wilen, Pierre Michelot and the Britons Victor Feldman, Cleo Laine and John Dankworth. West Indians include Joe Harriott, Harold McNair and Dizzy Reece.

11. The Alchemist, *Jazzwise*, June 2002.
12. Interview with the author, 2005.
13. Sleeve notes of Lawrence D. 'Butch' Morris *Current Trends in Racism in Modern America* (Sound Aspects, 1986).
14. Stanley Crouch, sleeve notes of Wynton Marsalis *Black Codes (From the Underground),* (Columbia, 1985)
15. Geoffrey Himes, 'The New Standard', *Jazz Times*, 1 May 2002.
16. Interview with the author, 2005.
17. Interview with the author, 2001.
18. Interview with the artist, 2023.
19. *Ibid.*
20. A key entry in Harper's songbook, 'Croquet Ballet' features on *Black Saint* (Black Saint, 1975).
21. In 2023 Ezra Collective, which includes drummer and leader Femi Koleoso, became the first jazz act to win the Mercury Music Prize.
22. Brazilian drummer Mariá Portugal, accompanist to avant-garde icon Anthony Braxton, among others, was nominated for the prestigious 2025 Deutscher Jazz Preis.
23. Jazz is not primarily marketed as dance music, but it can still make people dance. I'm not referring to only groups that use explicit dance rhythms such as funk, salsa or afrobeat but also to avant-garde artists whose music can draw physical as well as emotional responses from audiences.

ALSO AVAILABLE IN THIS SERIES